Constructive Talk in Challenging Classroo

How do you build trust and develop positive relationships in even the most challenging classrooms?

Constructive Talk in Challenging Classrooms gives the practising teacher advice on how to make learning fun through the use of 'talk' and collaborative group work. Using clear examples, tried and tested in some of the most challenging classrooms in inner-city schools, the book offers practical and honest advice on both the difficulties and rewards that can be gained when employing all forms of talk-based teaching in the classroom.

Packed with real examples of successful talk-based lessons with children of all abilities and needs, this book will show teachers how they can succeed in overcoming problems of disruption and engage even the most difficult pupils in real learning through talk.

Constructive Talk in Challenging Classrooms shows that bringing the child's individual experience into a lesson through talk has huge emotional and psychological benefits – this can be particularly marked in classrooms where there are low levels of literacy, behaviour issues or where pupils' first language is not English. The author argues that talk is vital for building positive relationships and essential for successful teaching, particularly in difficult classrooms.

This inspiring title is essential reading for any teacher interested in building trust and making learning fun and meaningful for all.

Valerie Coultas taught English and Humanities for more than two decades in London schools. She has been a Head of English and an Assistant Head teacher. She is now a senior lecturer in English at the School of Education, Kingston University.

Constructive Talk in Challenging Classrooms

Strategies for behaviour management and talk-based tasks

Valerie Coultas

Routledge
Taylor & Francis Group

LONDON AND NEW YORK

First published 2007
by Routledge
2 Park Square, Milton Park, Abingdon, Oxon OX14 4RN

Simultaneously published in the USA and Canada
by Routledge
270 Madison Ave, New York, NY 10016

Reprinted 2008

Routledge is an imprint of the Taylor & Francis Group,
an informa business

Typeset in Galliard by
RefineCatch Limited, Bungay, Suffolk
Printed and bound in Great Britain by
MPG Books Ltd, Bodmin, Cornwall

British Library Cataloguing in Publication Data
A catalogue record for this book is available from the British Library

Library of Congress Cataloging in Publication Data
Coultas, Valerie, 1951–
    Constructive talk in challenging classrooms : strategies for
behaviour management and talk-based tasks / Valerie Coultas.
        p.   cm.
    Includes bibliographical references and index.
    ISBN 0–415–40342–1   ISBN 0–415–40343–X   1. Learning.
2. Oral communication.   3. Oral communication—
Study and teaching.   I. Title.
LB1060.C69   2007
371.102′2—dc22   2006018400

ISBN10: 0–415–40342–1 (hbk)
ISBN10: 0–415–40343–X (pbk)
ISBN10: 0–203–96741–0 (ebk)

ISBN13: 978–0–415–40342–9 (hbk)
ISBN13: 978–0–415–40343–6 (pbk)
ISBN13: 978–0–203–96741–6 (ebk)

To all the pupils I have taught, and particularly those very naughty boys, who made teaching so difficult, such a challenge and such fun.

Contents

Figures

Acknowledgements

My thanks to Diana Webb, Janet Koike, Paul Blum and Ken Jones for their comments on drafts of this book.

Introduction

> Thought is not begotten by thought; it is engendered by motivation, i.e., by our desires, needs, interests and emotions.
>
> Vygotsky (1986)

The value of talk

This book is about talk. It will argue that constructive talk is one of the most essential ingredients of a good lesson, that talk is vital to engage any student in their learning, that talk can transform relationships in the classroom. It will also show teachers *how* to use talk-based activities in any classroom – even the most difficult ones.

Lessons that encourage and organise pupils to talk about their learning are not easy lessons to teach but, if successful, they are highly stimulating for pupils and teachers alike. Teachers require courage, expertise about how pupils' learn and determination to engage in this type of pedagogy, particularly in the most challenging classrooms.

Many teachers view the idea of collaborative talk positively but they have a natural inclination to avoid pupil talk in pairs and groups because they fear loss of control. In challenging schools the battle for control is not easy. Teachers can face constant verbal and non-verbal interruption, even direct defiance and personal insults. There are some classrooms and groups where even getting the pupils to sit down can be a triumph! Classrooms like this exist in many schools, particularly in lower and mixed ability groupings in non-selective comprehensive schools and in the later years of some primary schools. While teachers may have child-centred aspirations for their lessons, the fear of 'off-task' talk often means a retreat into the transmission mode of teaching. This is where the teacher directs the lesson and the pupils work on the same individual task. Whatever the experts say, it appears to be the only way to get the job done.

Thus the teacher has to have a very clear plan and structure for their lessons to initiate small group talk successfully. They need to know when and how to use collaborative talk. They need to be able to fully engage the pupils, give guidance and establish routines that tutor the pupils to learn cooperatively.

Talk can become a very successful part of the teacher's armoury, even in challenging circumstances. In fact, the pupils' language is an easily available resource that the teacher can use in any classroom. It is through thinking, talking and interacting with others that our capacity to learn increases. If carried out effectively, structured talk for a real purpose gives a teacher a more organic form of 'control' because the teacher is encouraging the pupils to use their language to make sense of new information. Pupils feel more secure when they have been able to express themselves and actively negotiate and construct their own meanings. This promotes new and different relationships, a more equal dialogue between the teacher and the pupils. It encourages pupils to see collaboration as the key to learning and to value ideas that come from each other as well as from the teacher.

Talk allows pupils to express doubts and clarify understanding; it legitimises the discussion of feelings, emotions and preferences. It makes learning more affective, more personal. It brings the school closer to the home by allowing the natural talk of the pupils to find a place in the classroom. This book will insist that it is not only the cognitive impact of talk on learning that is important. The psychological and social impact of talk can have a particularly dramatic impact on pupil motivation, particularly in challenging classrooms, because talk boosts children's self-esteem and helps to establish relationships based on respect. If it is structured effectively, talk can help the teacher relax and bring the fun and pleasure back into any classroom.

Having taught in several particularly challenging inner-city comprehensives, I know that all children show more enthusiasm for learning when teachers encourage them to talk. It may be necessary to start slowly and be careful to train pupils in how to answer closed and open questions, how to listen and talk to the teacher, how to listen and talk to each other, how to make presentations to the class or the school assembly. It may be necessary to start in small bouts of talk linked to reading or writing. But when a teacher allows the pupils to talk, and starts from what they already know about a subject, they feel more involved, more comfortable and less anxious and alienated. There is less likelihood of their being off task when they are allowed to use their imaginations in their learning and refer to their own cultural experiences. If pupils are allowed to ask the teacher questions and make observations about the subject or about how they are learning, and use their higher-order skills of evaluation, empathy and speculation, they will feel more in control and learning will take place at a deeper level.

It is in such lessons that the submerged talent of so many pupils is revealed. The oral skills of many pupils are often much more developed than their reading or writing. Pupils' oral ability often shows their real potential and can support them in developing their reading and writing skills. Students' insights on cultural and moral issues are often fresh and inspiring. When we articulate our thoughts or doubts we show that we understand or want to know more. When we compare what we already know with something new, we are really learning. Oracy is a key launching pad for learning and should have a central place in every classroom in the land.

Where there are lower sets in schools, the pupils will often surprise the teacher who takes the risk with pupil-led talk. Sometimes the pupils placed in the lower sets are so pleased to be given the chance to use their imaginations that they will be much more inventive than the top set. A wide variety of well-organised talk, with the emphasis on group achievement, allows pupils to show the teacher what they know and avoids the 'failure syndrome'. Sometimes there are so many children wanting to be in the hot seat that the exercise has to continue into the next lesson. There are moments of rapt attention, a common smile in a class where a joke is shared during a language game. However difficult or challenging the child or the group, the teacher will find that greater trust is established and their lessons are valued if they can create a classroom that talks to learn.

In many ways, talk-based lessons are most important in urban schools in 'challenging circumstances', where a high proportion of children are entitled to free school meals, where many children have English as an Additional Language (EAL) or pupils are still learning to read, where children are socially disadvantaged. The variety of language introduced and the way it is introduced, through demonstration and scaffolding, allows pupils to extend their language skills. Talk-based lessons validate the pupils' own language and culture, as well as recognising and developing a wide range of talk repertoires. A variety of talk-based activities extends the learning of pupils who have difficulties with reading and writing through joint planning and oral rehearsal to support the reading or writing task. Exploratory talk in small groups allows pupils to deepen understanding and develop thinking. Talk allows pupils from different cultural backgrounds greater freedom to express themselves and bring their knowledge and experience into the classroom. Talk can create space for working-class students, girls and boys, to explain a different view of the world. It recognises the validity of different forms of knowledge. It acts to celebrate language diversity in the classroom. Lessons based on well-structured talk, because they create a space for different roles, different inputs and different opinions, are naturally differentiated and inclusive.

How teachers can use talk successfully in challenging classrooms

This book will consider how educational policy has influenced the classroom teacher's attitude to talking and learning in small groups and interactive lessons and then describe, in some detail, how to set up different kinds of talk tasks and forms of group discussion in the classroom. The book will use a model of learning in small groups based on the work of the National Oracy Project to underpin the chapters. This project, which began in 1986, involved a wide range of teachers, advisors and researchers working together to establish good practice in encouraging small-group talk and effective forms of classroom discussion. Norman (2002) in *Thinking Voices* describes the work of the National Oracy Project. The process of planning for talk reflects a particular method and approach to teaching and involves teachers developing a view of themselves as facilitators of learning. Such a view requires teachers to plan carefully, sharing good practice with one another, and to consider how pupils learn rather than simply focusing on what they are learning. It involves facilitating pupils' learning through the stages of *engagement*, *exploration, transformation, presentation* and *review* (see table). These stages can inform lesson plans or longer-term plans.

The chapters start with the most natural kinds of classroom talk – teacher talk, reading aloud and questioning at the *engagement* stage. The chapters then move into short paired talk tasks at the *exploration* stage. Later chapters deal with group work, storytelling and drama where students *explore, transform* and *present* what they know. The chapters end on *reflection* and *assessment of talk*.

Once a teacher becomes familiar with this overall approach, they will be able to use the model flexibly as a planning aide to ensure that they prepare interactive lessons. The division of the chapters is aimed at giving teachers a framework to change their classroom practice, a

A model for small group learning

Engagement
Students encounter new information or engage in an experience that provides the basis for their learning.

Exploration
The students explore the new information.

Transformation
Students are required to use their understanding to work with the information to make decisions.

Presentation
The students present their findings to an interested audience.

Reflection
Students look at what they have learned and the process they have gone through.

Source: This figure is derived from information found in Cook, J, Forrestral P and Reid, J (1989) *Small Group Learning in the Classroom*, Chalkface Press.

structure for ensuring that their planning for speaking and listening is coherent.

The natural tendency of the secondary and top junior teacher, faced with a turbulent class, is, unsurprisingly, to close them down and set the pupils to work, e.g. after brief instructions they have to start writing. This book does not condemn the teacher for this practice or operate on a deficit model of teachers. Nor does it suggest that lessons where mainly writing takes place are a problem. If the writing task requires a short stimulus, or has been planned in previous lessons, this can be a completely valid approach. If a teacher wants pupils just to write, just to talk or just to read there should be space for this. In other lessons teachers will want to integrate the three strands of English in their planning. This book is not aimed at judging teachers but hopes to stand shoulder to shoulder with the classroom teacher and give helpful advice on how to plan for some form of interactivity in even the most difficult lessons.

The difficulties of carrying out small group activities in real classrooms are understood and acknowledged and each chapter tries to identify and discuss how to overcome potential problems. Each chapter will summarise the advice given. A model for whole staff training will be outlined and consideration will be given to issues of gender and special educational needs (SEN) in planning and assessing talk. The book will also recommend teaching materials that give good advice on talk.

Many of the tasks described have been used successfully in the most challenging inner-city schools, for example all-boys' schools in London in areas of social deprivation. They have been tried out and adapted over two decades of teaching in a number of different schools.

There are, of course, many elements to be balanced for a successful oral lesson. The teacher has to create the right climate for learning in this way. Establishing a climate for speaking and listening in challenging contexts might include the following:

- Being ready for the pupils and greeting them on arrival
- Talking about direct experience and encouraging pupils to do the same
- Encouraging students to work in pairs and small groups and training them to share and value each other's ideas and opinions
- Setting up informal debates and panels to encourage students to express their opinions and giving them a chance to speak to different audiences
- Allowing students to become involved in peer mentoring or reading projects with younger students
- Talking one-to-one with the pupils about the lesson and about other issues of interest to them
- Making it clear why speaking and listening are important and recording and rewarding pupils for progress in this strand
- Using different arrangements of furniture, different rooms for different activities, and different equipment, e.g. tape recorders, video cameras and ICT, to record and develop oral skills
- Using open-ended questions and allowing pupils to do the same
- Encouraging pupils to evaluate their learning and showing pupils that you will adapt your teaching as a result of their feedback
- Talking about how we learn and establishing ground rules for talk.

Classroom experience is never as neat as the textbooks suggest and the raucous behaviour of adolescent and pre-adolescent pupils will always be there to challenge and upset the best-laid plans. Teachers in challenging schools need the best and most practical advice they can find, combining different areas of educational expertise, to deal with the complex problems they face each day. There are no easy or quick-fix solutions in these settings.

This book therefore will establish the links between developing skills in planning for speaking and listening and the building of good relationships with students. The latter requires a teacher planning for talk to have a real understanding of the importance of positive reinforcement for these students and to be able to use and develop best practice in behaviour management.

Chapter 1

Talk under attack?

An overview of the debate

A chronology of talk's place in the curriculum

A creative phase for talk?

1965   Andrew Wilkinson coins the word 'oracy'

1967   The Plowden Report puts the child at the centre of the educational process and states that spoken language plays a central role in learning

1969   Publication of *Language, the Learner and the School* by Barnes, Britton and Rosen

1973   Action research groups on oracy in primary schools

1974   Bullock Report, *A Language for Life*, suggests that language competence grows through the interaction of writing, talk, reading and experience

1977   Harold Rosen, while at London University, establishes an archive of recordings celebrating the rich variety of pupils' language

1986   National Oracy Project established

The battle begins?

1987   National Curriculum Task Group on Assessment and Testing, chaired by Professor Paul Black, produces new recommendations for assessment that include a ten-point scale for measuring standards in English

1988   The Kingman Report puts forward a model of the English language in use and makes recommendations for the teaching of knowledge about language in Initial Teacher Training

1989   Language in the National Curriculum (LINC) project set up to develop teaching materials to improve knowledge about language

1989 The Cox Report suggests that the three strands of English, Speaking and Listening, Reading and Writing, should be of equal value

1990 National Curriculum created five attainment targets (four at Key Stage 3), later changed to three. Speaking and Listening was a separate and equal component of the curriculum. An integrated approach emphasised

1991 LINC teaching materials censored by Tim Eggar (Minister of State)

1992 Ofsted established

1993 *National Curriculum Council* (NCC) publishes *National Curriculum English: The Case for Revising the Order*

1993 SATS tests introduced based on assessing of reading and writing at Key Stages 1, 2, 3. Widespread boycott of Key Stage 3 tests

1995 Following the Dearing Review a slimmed down version *English in the National Curriculum* is published by the DfE

1996 National Literacy Task Force introduced the principle of National Literacy targets

1996–8 National Literacy Project

1998 National Literacy Strategy and Framework for Teaching focused on reading and writing

A new, eclectic phase?

2000 Curriculum 2000 – schools should cover three strands of English

2003 Qualifications and Curriculum Authority Conference on 'The Grammar of Talk'

2003 Excellence and Enjoyment

2003 Primary and Secondary National Strategies introduced, incorporating the National Numeracy Strategy and the National Literacy Strategy

2003 QCA issues new materials on Speaking and Listening

(Source: This chronology has been adapted and developed from information in Cox, B (1996) *Cox on the Battle for the English Curriculum*.)

The inclusion of speaking and listening as a separate profile component in our recommendations reflected the working group's conviction that they are of central importance to children's development. The value of talk in all subjects as a means of promoting pupils' understanding, and of evaluating their progress, is now widely understood.

Cox, B (1991)

There has been much talk about talk in the debate on the English curriculum. This chapter attempts to assess the impact of these debates on classroom teachers.

Speaking and listening has often been called 'the Cinderella strand' because, compared with the reading and writing strands, it is the most easily cast aside. This book openly acknowledges that many teachers find this aspect of teaching English a challenge but this chapter also raises questions about the consistency of the advice given by policy makers. It considers whether the present system of examinations helps schools and teachers accord an equal role to speaking and listening in their planning. For those teachers who have sought to embed speaking and listening within the English curriculum and other subjects, the advice has sometimes seemed inconsistent. When working in urban schools, where talk can help to empower pupils who need to develop greater self-confidence with language use, these policy changes can have an important impact.

The creative phase: the arrival of pupil-led talk

The word 'oracy' became part of our vocabulary in 1965 when Andrew Wilkinson argued that a third dimension should be added to the conception of the educated person. They should be numerate, literate and 'orate'.

He argued that 'oracy' was not a 'subject' but 'a condition of learning in all subjects' (Wilkinson, 1965). He insisted that oracy was fundamental to learning: 'Its encouragement is a matter of the fundamental attitudes of the school towards its pupils; of their relationship with the staff; of the degree of responsibility accorded them; of the confidence they acquire . . .' (ibid.). Nancy Martin made this point even more succinctly when she argued that 'writing and reading float on a sea of talk' (cited in Corden, 1988).

With the publication of *Language, the Learner and the School* (Barnes, Britton and Rosen, 1969), the value of the home language of the child, referred to as 'real' talk, was established and teachers were urged to use that language to allow for real learning through social interaction in the classroom. The social constructivist view of these authors suggested that learning was a social experience and that exploratory talk in small groups was vital to scaffold the learning of pupils and move them on to a new stage. The suggestion was that informal talk was vital to learning and not simply the formal language of instruction. These ideas were central to many teacher-training programmes in the 1970s and early 1980s and still retain some importance today.

The debate on oracy at this time ran parallel to but sometimes at odds with the desire to find means of assessing spoken English. The writers who saw oracy as integral to learning and reading and writing had reservations about the formal assessment of spoken English. But others saw formal oral assessment as part of the drive to incorporate the 'O' level and the CSE into the GCSE to cater for all abilities. As Graham Frater (1988) points out it was early CSE listening comprehension texts, not the 'O' level that had reflected an oral tradition, for 'oracy was largely excluded for the more prestigious GCE O level examination in English'.

We can see the origins of the present GCSE English curriculum in Wilkinson's suggestions that pupils should be given the opportunity to 'discuss, to negotiate, to converse' with a range of audiences, 'their fellows, with the staff, with other pupils'.

Frater goes on to point out the difficulties with oral assessment and criticised the generally poor quality of the test materials. He suggested that the new GCSE should assess speaking and listening in a different way – 'by making oral assessment genuinely continuous; in training teachers appropriately . . . and then in trusting them without further moderation or validation' (1988).

This is close to the present system for assessing speaking and listening at age 16 in the GCSE English exam. Although teachers have spot checks on the internal moderation procedures, this is the one part of the curriculum where a teacher's judgement is accepted. But the formative assessment of oracy has never been given the same attention as the summative exams which test writing.

Harold Rosen, while at London University, collected an archive of recordings and transcripts which documented the influences of different regional dialects on speech. His work celebrated the richness of accent and dialect and the great variety of the English oral tradition. This, alongside Wilkinson's challenge to the domination of writing as the key mode of learning, constituted an assault on educational tradition. These developments suggested that pupil talk assisted all forms of learning and that accents other than received pronunciation should be valued. They established the groundwork for a holistic approach to language development and English teaching.

The Bullock Report on oral language made a clear statement of the key principles of the relationship between oracy and literacy and suggested that 'the point to be emphasized is that the child's language should be accepted' (DES, 1975: 143).

In primary schools, during this period, Joan Tough (1973) promoted the ideas of the Bullock Report by establishing action-research groups in which teachers worked together to reflect on their own practice in speaking and listening and its impact on their pupils.

The work of teachers, LEAs and LEA advisers led to the Schools Development Curriculum establishing the National Oracy Project in 1986 – a project that was established to develop initiatives that promoted oracy in the school curriculum.

In primary schools inspectors found 'many opportunities provided for talk and listening; books, writing and practical work have all been noted as stimulating and focusing talk particularly effectively'. According to Frater (1988), inspectors also found 'that the disposition of furniture could play a significant part in the effectiveness, or otherwise of the spoken word'.

In secondary schools, according to inspectors, the picture was sketchier. At this stage, in 1987, inspectors report that the spoken word is 'generally undervalued in the teaching of English' and across the curriculum 'the general picture of the spoken word shows fewer signs of movement' (Frater, 1988). But reports did indicate 'instances of good practice' in English lessons and these had the following features: 'The variation of group sizes; clear purposes; simulation activities; good links with reading activities. . . . Drama . . . was noted as prompting confident talk when it was planned' (ibid.).

In urban areas such as London, there were, by the mid-1980s, networks of English and English as an Additional Language (EAL) teachers who were attempting to develop good practice in speaking and listening and allow pupils' home language and culture a presence in schools. Some of these teachers believed that working-class culture had expressive forms, both orally and in writing, and the job of the teacher was to unlock that potential and give form to that cultural expression. Classroom teachers in areas such as Tower Hamlets, for example, were incorporating myths and legends from other cultures into their reading practices to address the needs of the multilingual pupils they taught, to encourage pupil response and interpretation of texts. Rex Gibson was pioneering active approaches to Shakespeare through drama and choric reading and drama and storytelling workshops became an established practice in many schools. The collaborative learning project was established in 1986 to promote interactive resources that could address the language needs of EAL pupils. Media Studies was being introduced in English classrooms enabling pupils to discuss and analyse a wider range of texts, 'texts' they were sometimes even more familiar with than their teachers.

The Inner London Education Authority (ILEA) English Centre at this time was helping to establish networks of teachers and publishing innovative materials that planned for speaking and listening and pupil response. It also published excellent samples of pupils' writing from a wide range of cultural perspectives. Jon Davidson, writing in the *TES* (2004), praised the work of the ILEA in supporting newly qualified, probationary English teachers, celebrating the 'linguistic and cultural richness in London'. He said that 'Contact with current research and thinking did so much for our self-esteem. . . . Those ILEA teacher centres planted a passion in me, and I'd like modern NQTs to have the same advantage'.

So, although many teachers would still have practised more traditional modes of teaching, by the end of the 1980s there was, according to Frater, strong support 'for the enhancement of the spoken word and a clear appreciation of its importance in the learning process'. Among teachers of pupils with EAL, concentrated in urban areas, there was a growing understanding of the importance of collaborative learning to promote language development.

English in the National Curriculum (DES, 1990) allocated a prominent role to talk in the primary and secondary classroom. While there were many debates among teachers about the Coxian literary canon (an implicit one at this stage) potentially restricting the choice of texts, and controversies over the importance of Standard English, the new document did validate at least some of the arguments that had been made for including oracy as part of the English curriculum. Speaking and Listening became first among equals as Attainment Target One in the documentation. An integrated approach to planning for speaking and listening, reading and writing was advocated.

Talk under attack: SATS, league tables and literacy targets arrive

The move towards promoting a curriculum rich in pupil-led talk was initially developed by pupils, teachers, LEA advisers and teacher trainers working together to invent new approaches to teaching. The policy makers gave recognition to this work in the English National Curriculum by including Speaking and Listening as the first of three strands. The Language in the National Curriculum (LINC) project was established in 1989 to develop teacher knowledge of how spoken and written language worked and to ensure that teachers fully understood the implications of the changes in the National Curriculum.

However, the materials from the LINC project, based on an approach that trained teachers to value what their pupils already knew about language, were suppressed. According to Cox (1996) the English Curriculum was subject to a takeover by a 'small, extreme right-wing group' (p. 29) who advocated a return to traditional grammar teaching and was 'contemptuous towards the professional teacher' (p. 25). The Conservative Government was beginning to develop a standards agenda that took debates about English teaching in a different direction.

According to Ken Jones (1989), the philosophical basis for the attack came from the authors of the Black papers who had been developing a critique of modern English teaching. The attack was made on the child-centred nature of English teaching. The authors of the papers argued that English teaching was about imparting a body of knowledge, which involved re-establishing English literary heritage and the explicit teaching of grammar and Standard English, and that standards would only be maintained in schools if they were clearly and publicly defined. Sheila Lawlor spelt out what she felt was wrong with progressive teaching methods with her remark that there was 'no reason to suggest that pupils learn from talking' (cited in Jones, 1989). This view directly challenged the idea that learning was a social experience and instead emphasised the need for direct instruction.

Alongside the debate around the English National Curriculum, therefore, parallel developments allowed concern over standards to lead to the establishment of new structures that would take the debate out of the hands of the specialists. The National Literacy Task Force was established in 1987 under the stewardship of Professor Paul Black. This task force was focused on the need to raise attainment through developing more rigorous forms of assessment and clearly defining different levels of attainment in English.

The standards agenda now developed several clear projects: establishing literacy targets for schools and LEAs, ensuring that standards were clear by creating new public exams in the form of standardised reading and writing tests (SATS) in English at ages 7, 11, and 14; and guaranteeing that standards were publicly defined through the controversial league tables to be published in the national press, a further method of driving up standards. Ofsted was also established in 1992 to ensure that schools were following the standards agenda. At a later stage, school improvement theories began to impose an even tighter managerial framework on schools as performance management was promoted and heads were encouraged to set numerical targets for individual teachers, particularly those teaching core subjects such as English, Maths and Science.

The National Literacy Task Force developed the National Literacy Project and this became the National Literacy Strategy of the new Labour Government. The National Curriculum gave schools guidance over what they should teach, and the revised order in 1995 included a hotly debated prescribed list of texts, a canon, that explicitly defined the 'English literary heritage'. The National Literacy Strategy now laid down direct instructions on how English or literacy should be taught, taking control over pedagogy with a manual of objectives for each term and each year. This context therefore influenced the aims of the National Literacy Strategy. The findings of the pilot studies, which suggested there should be more room for teacher initiative, were not incorporated into the final document. The primary focus was to raise standards in reading and writing by giving teachers very precise guidelines and objectives as to how to teach English.

The National Literacy Strategy, introduced in 1998, was aimed at raising standards in literacy. It required teachers to set clear learning objectives based on a manual of objectives for each year group from reception to year 9. The literacy hour in primary school was divided into four parts. The teacher had to introduce a text in the first quarter of the lesson, following this up with word- or sentence-level work to ensure that grammar was being taught explicitly. The third part of the hour was devoted to individual or group work and the final session was the plenary, when the teacher was urged to check that the learning outcomes had been fulfilled. At Key Stage 3 the hour was adapted to begin with a starter activity and then lead into an introduction.

There are many different views expressed among educational practitioners on the National Literacy Strategy (NLS) and its impact in schools. The Labour Government claimed that the strategy resulted in higher standards in literacy. By 2005, 4 out of 5 pupils were leaving primary schools with at least average levels of literacy. Gemma Moss (2004) in a study that considers the impact of the NLS on classroom practice suggests that the pace and shape of literacy teaching has changed, leading to much 'stronger teacher control over the pace and sequence of activity'. Many have tried to work with the documentation, focusing on its strengths and stressing, for example, the positive features of the strategy in promoting interactive whole-class teaching. Angela Wilson (2001) asserts her views very strongly when she says: 'I have heard it said recently that the literacy hour "has put speaking and listening on the back burner". This is nonsense'.

Many teachers in schools have also adopted a pragmatic view, picking out the parts of the strategy they find most useful such as encouraging pupils to read and write a wider range of non-fiction texts and using shared reading, where the class reads aloud together, and shared writing, where the teacher writes in front of the class, to model and scaffold the learning of pupils. When the Key Stage 3 National Strategy documentation (2001) argued that literacy skills should be made part of 'the explicit teaching agenda in all classrooms' this proved useful for, once again, raising awareness of the need for all teachers to regard themselves as teachers of English. It also gave many heads the opportunity to appoint literacy coordinators to take more concrete steps to assist staff in, for example, creating more literacy-aware classrooms.

However, there were also many who have raised doubts about the National Literacy Strategy. Speaking and listening was not accorded equal status with reading and writing in the NLS framework for primary teachers. As Wyse and Jones (2001) point out, 'speaking and listening activities are located as a subsidiary within wider work on reading and writing'. They point out that there is 'an implicit suggestion that speaking and listening activities are more suited to key stage one'. They also suggest that the function of talk is different in the framework than in the National Curriculum. 'Speaking and listening take on a functional quality; a means by which the skills of reading and writing may be enhanced.'

Yet the exploratory and investigative forms of talk that are undervalued in the NLS framework are vital for developing pupil motivation, confidence, understanding and ability to think at any age. As Barnes et al. (1969) in *Language, the Learner and the School* pointed out so clearly: 'We sharpen our understanding by telling or attempting to explain to others. . . . Without plentiful experience of talking things through we would be denied access to that inner speech through which we organize our thinking'.

Despite claims that the NLS was based on interactive teaching, the advice given to primary teachers in the *Framework for Teaching* (DES, 1998) on speaking and listening was at best inadequate to support teachers in planning for this strand.

George Hunt (2001) also takes up the theme of limiting pupil response in analysing a transcript of a National Literacy Strategy training video (DFEE, 1998): 'Most of the teacher–pupil interactions featured in its training video conform to the Initiation-Response-Evaluation (IRE) pattern long recognised as a typical and intrinsically limiting form of classroom interaction'.

Heads of English, while in training sessions in Croydon in London, for example, as the Key Stage 3 strategy was being introduced in 2001, also raised questions about shared writing sessions on training videos where the teacher's role seemed very didactic and there were few choices involved in writing tasks. There was an underlying unease among experienced English teachers about the approach embedded in the strategy. The focus seemed to be on compensating for what working-class pupils lacked, rather than building on their existing language competencies to acquire new skills. The emphasis did seem to be placed more on direct instruction.

George Hunt (2001) argues that with the National Literacy Strategy 'the educational establishment's insistence on prescriptive curricula and measurable outcomes has demonstrated the vulnerability of exploratory talk'. He suggests that 'the vagaries of such talk, not to mention that it takes time away from direct teaching, are barely tolerated under a regime that values a "sense of urgency" in classrooms'. Gemma Moss (2004) suggests that the fast pace of lesson planning to cover multiple objectives gave teachers little time to ensure that pupils had really been able to transfer knowledge gained from word-level work into their independent writing.

These arguments imply that the attack on talk was not necessarily a deliberate one. Rather, that talk has been one particular casualty of the standards agenda, first imposed by the Conservative Government, and the drive towards centralisation in education that the Labour Government has overseen in the last decade. The National Literacy Strategy was introduced in a very centralised manner, particularly in primary schools, where an army of literacy consultants arrived with manuals and stop watches in hand to ensure that the literacy hour was delivered exactly as suggested by the DFES. The increasing centralisation of the British education system is a process that others, such as Robin Alexander (2000), have commented on. Lessons based around small group talk require the teacher to take the initiative in planning and to make judgements about the pupils they teach and the strategies they use. Such an approach cannot be imposed from above.

It is evident that the documentation at Key Stage 3 did not make quite the same errors as that of the primary framework. Speaking and listening and drama objectives were included. Perhaps some lessons had been learnt from the reception given to the primary framework or perhaps the GCSE exam had helped to embed speaking and listening more firmly in secondary school practice? But the theoretical underpinning, as manifested both in the overall thrust of the documentation and the training videos, underlined the transmission mode of teaching and the analysis of the linguistic features of the text to improve reading and writing. Thomas (2001) added his voice to those who had doubts, suggesting that the pleasure in reading and writing was being lost: 'the emphasis is increasingly upon what the child must do to be acceptable to the adult world. This will make form and presentation more important than attitude, feeling and purpose'. Others, such as Smith and Hardman (2000), warned that the literacy strategy was not addressing children with special needs. The fast pace and didactic form of lessons, and the lack of time for exploratory talk, did not necessarily create a climate in which these pupils would flourish.

The third phase: an eclectic change of heart?

Ironically, some members of the new inspection regime (Ofsted), established to drive forward the standards agenda, produced evidence that highlighted the errors in the dominant mode of pedagogy underlying the National Literacy Strategy. Educational researchers had already begun to identify problems through analysing teachers concerns, which revealed doubts about the importance given to speaking and listening, drama and the focus on short extracts, rather than whole texts, as the basis for teaching.

The teacher's role in questioning also became the subject of research. The pressure on teachers to check learning outcomes was encouraging closed rather than open questioning techniques. A survey on the literacy hour by the Institute of Education (Riley and Elmer, 2001) revealed that of an average of 75 questions:

25 per cent were closed
25 per cent were asked in a way that should involve simple deduction or
    paraphrasing
20 per cent were simple recall of data
13 per cent were pseudo-questions to do with classroom management
Only 4 per cent encouraged children to express feelings or show empathy
5 per cent encouraged higher-order thinking skills
3 per cent required students to support their answer with reference to
    the text.

These statistics further highlight some problems with the advice inherent in the strategy. Focusing exclusively on the form rather than the meaning of the text will always lead to a greater emphasis on closed questions, spotting linguistic features. R. Bunting (2000) makes the point that this is not the best way to teach grammar. Her view is that grammar should be introduced in an understood context and, reaffirming the approach advocated in the LINC project, she states: 'the important pedagogic principle about the teaching of terminology is that a pattern of experience needs to be established before the term is introduced'. A focus on the experience and use of language and the meaning of a text will allow pupils to build on their existing knowledge and move towards a greater shared understanding of a text and more open responses. Terminology is then introduced in a relevant context.

The underestimation of the value of collaborative and explorative talk and the role of the teacher in promoting pupil discussion and response were not the only errors made in the advice given to teachers in the National Literacy Strategy. As suggested above there were many other questions raised. Primary teachers soon began to realise that, within the strict timescale of the literacy hour, there was little time for children to engage in a sustained piece of reading or writing. To complete such tasks schools had to add time for more extended writing.

The lack of flexibility meant that neither the needs of the most able nor those with special needs were particularly well catered for within the literacy hour. Teachers also began to address the problem of short extracts by opting to study whole texts and plan over a two- or three-week period, stressing the importance of engaging the class with a complete narrative. The mechanisms that teachers had chosen to use, for example the process approach to writing – where pupils plan together, collaborate on a draft, re-write and try out their work on an audience – could actually be undermined by the rigid timings of the literacy hour. The NLS also seemed to downplay the importance of media texts and ICT in English teaching. As R. Bennett (2004) points out:

> Although there is very clear and systematic guidance for teaching every aspect of literacy, the strategy makes very little mention of the role of ICT. Of the 16 references to ICT, six refer to spell checkers and the rest focus on presentation such as bullet pointing.

It is therefore probably not surprising that the DFES has started producing a great deal of supplementary materials to address some of these weaknesses. New documentation has been produced for primary schools on speaking and listening and drama (DFES, 2003a and e) and CD-ROM-based development packages provide guidance on Using ICT in the Literacy Hour. The new Key Stage 3 strategy documentation for the foundation subjects, *Pedagogy and Practice* (2003c), advises secondary teachers to use well-tried strategies for collaborative talk such as Jigsaw, Rainbow Groups and Snowballing.

Recent work by educational researchers has continued to advocate and develop a social constructivist view of learning. Neil Mercer (2000) has developed the debate on small group talk by arguing for dialogic learning. He offers suggestions for overcoming the problems of disputational talk by suggesting that teachers encourage pupils in groups to reason and discuss at a deeper level through establishing ground rules for talk. Roy Cordon (2000) has continued to develop the approach of the National Oracy Project in the primary classroom. Carter and McCarthy (1997) have developed the debate on talk repertoires by publishing transcripts of talk in different contexts. Robin Alexander (2004) has worked with LEAs to promote teaching through dialogue.

The *Excellence and Enjoyment* (DFES, 2003b) documentation, ironically, urges teachers 'to take ownership of the curriculum', telling teachers in primary schools that the literacy and numeracy strategies 'are not statutory' – that the classroom teacher can 'ignore/adapt; pick or choose' from the frameworks. The document also gives schools permission to 'decide the depth of study, length of lessons, whether subjects are taught discretely', opening the door to the kind of cross-curricular, creative planning that more experienced primary teachers are, unsurprisingly, rather familiar with. A recent HMI report (2005), while recognising that English and drama (when it is taught separately) are among the best subjects taught in schools, is also highly critical of 'teachers who have interpreted the NLS guidance inflexibly and, as a result, learning does not match the needs of pupils'. This report (2005) goes on to suggest that 'Planning for speaking and listening lacks rigour' and that 'Many schools pay too little attention to teaching the full National Curriculum programme of study for speaking and listening'.

Interestingly, the section on speaking and listening in this document includes no reference to the National Literacy Strategy. So teachers who based their plans on the needs of their pupils and the broader aims of the National Curriculum have, to some extent, been vindicated.

However, despite all the supplementary materials recognising some of the mistakes in the strategy, the SATS exams remain as written public exams linked to publicly defined standards as represented by the league tables. The DFES has stated that the SATS are a 'non-negotiable' part of the debate on English teaching. The tests place no real value on speaking and listening, unlike the GCSE English exam. There are few resources for training teachers to plan for small group work or participate in the formative assessment of oracy. This creates little space for creativity in a curriculum oriented to exams that remain highly traditional in form. The literacy targets remain in place and systems of performance management have become more embedded in schools. Pressure is put on schools in challenging circumstances to meet literacy targets. The new QCA speaking and listening materials have been utilised by some primary schools but many schools with league table position uppermost in their minds, have kept their weekly literacy plans, based exclusively on the NLS objectives, from the previous period.

The HMI report on English teaching (2005) identifies some key issues for English teachers and criticises some schools for lack of flexibility in their use of the NLS, for relying too heavily on textbooks and published materials and for the lack of attention given to drama, speaking and listening and reading for pleasure. But is it fair to place the blame on schools and teachers? Recent versions of the English Curriculum place less emphasis on reading for pleasure than earlier versions. Drama and speaking and listening require staff training, careful thought and planning to be taught effectively. Has the advice of the policy makers been consistent on speaking and listening? To do better in the tests and to gain a higher place in the league tables, schools and teachers are told to target the pupils most likely to boost results. Rather than plan lessons that directly address the needs of their pupils, teachers are urged to cover predetermined objectives. Instead of planning for their own forms of assessment, schools are pressured to concentrate on the optional tests and, often through direct instruction, practise reading comprehension and writing at the end of every single year. However, to teach English better we should value speaking and listening, drama, reading for pleasure and develop a more integrated and creative approach to English teaching. There are two distinct directions for English teaching here. Which one is correct?

In the more open forum created by *Excellence and Enjoyment*, it is time to reassert the creative value of pupil-based collaborative talk, the social nature of the learning process, and place the needs of the child right at the centre of English teaching. This is important in all classrooms. It is particularly important in urban comprehensive schools where socially disadvantaged pupils and students with EAL and special needs require the oral rehearsal and scaffolding that talk brings to reading and writing. It is the one in five children who fail to reach the national standard in literacy at age 11 who particularly benefit from lessons that value their culture and their oral language. For future generations, and for the most disadvantaged children, the change must not be just eclectic.

Chapter 2

Teacher talk

How to talk so they will listen

> My blood pressure has skyrocketed. I can feel the blood bubbling against my cheeks. My head is throbbing from the noise and humiliation of it all and still the class is not listening.
>
> Gilbert (2004)

A teacher's job involves a lot of talk. The classroom is very much a stage for the teacher's performance, yet there is often little discussion about how a teacher should act on this stage, how they should talk or read to the class. In difficult classrooms, like Mr Gilbert's, the key issue is often the battle to get the pupils' attention so that you *can* talk to the class. The two facets are linked together however. How you talk can also help you get their attention.

Getting the pupils settled

Paradoxically it is probably best if you don't talk too much at the very beginning of a lesson. Be ready for them by standing by the door, if possible. Be ready to briefly greet and acknowledge the pupils and ensure an orderly entry but wait to talk to the class as a whole. As the pupils arrive, and walk into the room sensibly, give them a task to complete that is self-evident – a starter or calmer – then when they are settled you begin your introduction.

Calmers and starters

To establish a good atmosphere at the beginning of the day, or the beginning of a lesson, it is a good idea to have a drill that involves pupils coming in and getting straight down to work. Michael Marland (1991), in *The Craft of the Classroom*, suggested starters or calming activities at the beginning of a lesson. He points out that many less experienced teachers, particularly in inner-city settings, lose the class in the first 5 minutes of the lesson. The Key Stage 3 literacy strategy also recommended starter activities for 10–15 minutes at the beginning of lessons. Many primary school teachers start their day with a period of silent, individual reading.

In the bustle of secondary schools, where pupils move from lesson to lesson in busy corridors, it is a very good idea for pupils to have something to do as soon as they arrive in a classroom, something that calms them down and focuses them on what they are about to learn. In challenging junior school classrooms, this approach at the beginning of a session or topic would also work well. This involves extra planning and sometimes means the production of a second set of materials by the teacher. Many classroom teachers' days are extraordinarily intensive and both physically and psychologically draining. A primary school teacher often arrives early to set up her classroom. In classrooms where pupils misbehave a lot, the teacher may have to keep several classes or individuals behind each day which will mean missing a large part of their break and some of their lunch hour. If lunch is short, 30 minutes in some secondary schools now, you can lose all your lunch hour. So producing an extra activity at the beginning requires careful thought and planning, in advance, so that it is not too much of a burden on the individual teacher. A calming activity can be very useful for establishing the right atmosphere for learning.

Learning support teachers and assistants can play an important role in assisting the teachers in producing materials. However, the school or the department will need to create time for the class teacher and the teaching assistant to work together on this. Some teaching resources that can be used as calmers or starters can be purchased but they are most likely to be tasks that are not integral to the lesson. The most realistic strategy for producing calmers is for teachers to think up ideas that can be a simple request or something that is written or projected onto a whiteboard. These ideas can be developed through teachers brainstorming together and sharing good practice. Pupils can be asked to write down the learning outcomes and the teacher will then hand them an exercise that revises the last lesson or links to the new learning in this lesson. Some suggestions might be:

- A list of words linked to the topic, with the definitions in the wrong order, can be handed out and pupils asked to correct them

- A set of anagrams they have to solve that link to the learning
- A cloze exercise based on a relevant text
- A crossword or grid linked to previously learnt concepts
- Words or sentences in the wrong order that they have to sequence
- A mind map or drawing to complete
- Words to put with pictures
- A piece of text to read silently and possibly annotate, e.g. by marking words that are new to the pupils or words/phrases that are powerful
- A piece of writing, which will be used later, that the pupils have to proofread
- A text to read in silence that is at their level
- Two or three points they can remember from the last lesson about. . . .

Something that is fairly self-evident as an exercise and needs little teaching, just a little interaction and some prompting to get started, is ideal. Then the teacher can take the register, check the exercise and introduce their lesson with the full attention of the class – including the latecomers!

Unlike the teacher who shouts at every latecomer in mid-sentence, you will be in a more relaxed position where you can actually take a note of the lateness, get the pupil working and try not to get too frustrated by these inevitable interruptions. Lateness can be punished at the end of the lesson, by helping you to clear up, if that is possible. Remember, the clash between latecomer and teacher is great entertainment for the pupils but it is a drain on you. When you decide to punish, make sure the pupils suffer rather than you.

By insisting on a quiet entry into the classroom and making it a drill or routine, you establish your room as a learning zone, as a place where pupils generally do not muck about. Praise, rather than negative declarations, can reinforce this routine. Clear, simple classroom rules can be very useful in giving clarity to your expectations of good listening. If the school has adopted such a system then make sure you use it. Some schools in challenging circumstances, however, have too many rules and pupils tend to ignore them. Suggestions might be:

1   Arrive on time
2   Listen to others
3   Work to the best of your ability.

Listing names on the board, to acknowledge cooperation with these basic rules, can act as a spur to creating a learning momentum. Even in a cover lesson, learning the names of those who want to cooperate by placing their names on the board will help you establish good relations quickly. You will surprise them by not starting off with a negative approach. You may wish to back up your entry drill with a seating plan but this is best done at the start of the year with a new class. You will need to teach the pupils that it is you who decides where they sit, but this can be hard to implement when you are new, unless it is general practice in the school. The calmer exercise and praise for following basic rules is, therefore, a very effective preparation for the opening of your lesson. It creates a sense of purpose and wins the majority of pupils over to your side straight away. Of course, as you gain more control, you will not have to be so rigid in your planning.

Getting everyone to listen to your introduction

Once the pupils are settled and you are ready for them to listen to you, cue them to listen by giving very clear, specific and polite instructions, saying 'put down your pens and look at me' and insist that everyone obeys you. When you ask the pupils to talk among themselves you will need to cue them back to you at this and at other points in the lesson. There are many cueing systems you can use. Some examples are:

- Say 'Pens down, eyes to the front' or something similar
- Count 1, 2, 3
- Clap your hands
- Tap with a coin
- Tap a tambourine or triangle
- Raise your arm and ask pupils to follow
- Chant and model an action rhyme, e.g. 'head, shoulders, eyes and nose look at me', for younger children.

Whatever you choose, use it systematically at key teaching moments and train the pupils to stop what they are doing and listen to you. Cueing gives you an alternative to the undignified 'shushing' that rarely works and makes you feel so ineffectual.

How to introduce your topic and lead the pupils into learning

If you have successfully cued the children to listen, wait for all of them to comply. Do not rush into speech. Pause for all to be alert and ready to listen to you. Less experienced teachers often fail to understand the importance of pauses and silence and the contribution these moments make to the classroom atmosphere. Dramatic pauses are very effective with classes if used at the right moment. You want to emphasise that this is an important moment in the lesson. Then you are ready to speak to them. Your audience is the children. Your purpose is to inform, entertain and engage all the pupils. If you make your introduction interesting for the children you are obviously going to keep their attention for longer. As soon as they start leaning back on their chairs you will know that you are losing them. Think about how you can relate to their experience, existing knowledge and sense of fun. The most successful lessons often make a connection between your experience, their experience and the topic. Remember what you were interested in at that age; what your children are interested in now. Try to focus on explanations that are memorable, that involve your audience in some way.

How to make your introduction interesting

You could start with a survey, e.g. how many languages can we say hello in? You may wish to use an anecdote or story. During a lesson on fear put the two ideas together by talking about what frightens you and then, after pupils have told a partner about their fears, carry out a class survey. This works well because it is *real* talk, about your personal fears, not just teacher talk. You are using talk not to direct or explain but to share an experience.

This notion of real talk, introduced by Douglas Barnes *et al.* (1969), suggested that children come to school with a wide range of experiences from their home. He argued that schools should use this home know-ledge to allow pupils to make connections between what they already know and the new forms of knowledge they have to acquire in school. It was the active making of connections that he believed was at the core of learning. These ideas influenced how teachers should teach, how they should use and value different types of language in the classroom and encouraged teachers and pupils to see learning as a social experience and encouraged pupils to talk to each other in small groups. Such an approach emphasises the importance of developing the expressive and imaginative modes of English teaching, which facilitate oral anecdote and storytelling and allow for the use of the language of feelings, fears and emotions that children bring into school from their lives at home.

Further suggestions for introducing a subject might be:

- Get the pupils to tell you what they already know about a new topic and what they want to know.
- Use a shared experience such as reflecting on a visit, an assembly theme, a TV programme or a past event that is relevant to your lesson.
- Use pupil or teacher in role to introduce a character or theme in a story, poem, play or even a non-fiction text as a pre-reading activity.
- Use a pupil to act out a conversation with a teacher to teach a new idea.
- Use pupil possessions as props by, for example, starting a discussion on advertising by asking pupils to show off any logos they have on their bags, clothes or equipment.
- Use some key words or pictures to get the pupils telling stories to each other.
- Ask pupils to write down a question they would like to ask about the last lesson.
- Introduce a new topic and ask pupils to discuss and come up with their own questions. The class can vote on the question they would like to discuss first.
- Get the pupils to discuss the themes, characters or setting before you start reading to them to generate enthusiasm for the written word.
- Use the pupils' own writing, drawing or recording to show what they have achieved already, to involve and engage them and to point them forward to the next steps.

Images, both still and moving, are also useful stimuli for talk:

- Try drawing an image or putting a picture or photograph on an OHP or interactive whiteboard to open up the discussion.
- Use a short video clip or piece of music to get pupils thinking.

You can also use listening exercises to focus pupils' attention.

- Get them to discuss or describe something in pairs and then tell the class what their partner said.

- Get them to repeat your instructions to the class.
- Ask them to draw some images that go through their mind as you are reading the first page or paragraph of the story or text.

Small moments that clearly illustrate the point are much more important for learning than endless dry speeches by the teacher. A sense of progress, success and achievement needs to be generated to motivate all learners but particularly reluctant learners. Teachers need to introduce the lesson with the audience, that is the pupils, in mind. Learning objectives can be mentioned but they will not, in most cases, inspire pupils in their own right. You have to engage pupils on a more personal level to make learning meaningful in challenging contexts.

Think about your audience

The National Literacy Strategy videos often showed children listening quietly and politely to very formal and teacher-centred language. Real children, with no TV crew and cameras present, are less likely to acquiesce so easily. In fact a large degree of the adolescent pupil's intellectual energy is concentrated on the repartee and banter between pupils and between pupils and teacher. The hidden classroom discourse and the agenda that pupils bring to the lesson runs parallel to the teacher's lesson aims. In challenging classrooms, pupils gain kudos for subverting the teacher's agenda. In many challenging contexts, and particularly in lower sets, the majority of the pupils are male. The teacher has to be adept at responding to these challenges and ignoring, incorporating or redirecting that energy towards the aims of the lesson.

A teacher in a real classroom therefore has to be very creative and responsive if they are to capture the adolescent pupil's interest and imagination and direct it towards the learning goals. You have to hook the pupils into the lesson and reinforce the learning goals as you explain the task. You can fix the objective in their mind through a story, anecdote, an example, a model or an illustration. Tell them how much you expect them to read or write and why you are asking them to do this and how you will be rewarding those that work hard. You have to give very clear, specific instructions and describe exactly what you want them to do but also have a light, personal touch.

Interruptions in the early stages of a lesson

In real classrooms, the problems come, of course, when you are inter-rupted. In challenging schools you often have to deal with multiple interruptions, not just one or two. Try to stay calm and emphasise that most pupils are listening to you or that the children near that pupil are listening to you and following the classroom rules. It is one of the con-tradictions of teaching that even the child who misbehaves repeatedly often really wants to please their teacher. Boys are often seeking atten-tion through misbehaviour. Show the class that you are going to give your attention to the pupils that work with you.

A little while after the interruption, try to diffuse the situation by asking the pupil a question that you think they can answer. Above all, avoid immediately addressing the individual loudly and negatively as this will escalate the confrontation. Deliberately ignoring misbehaviour is a key weapon in your armoury and pupils can understand that if you attain your overall goals. Repeat your instruction for the whole class. If the child is persistent in their misbehaviour give them a warning but, if possible, do this calmly and with authority. Sometimes, if you are able to move closer to that child and give the warning, then move away again you may get them settled. It may be possible to tell the child what you would like them to do as a choice and then walk away, giving them the opportunity to comply without losing status. Sometimes you can diffuse a potential con-frontation with a joke but never directly at the pupil's expense. If you do overreact, and all teachers do at some point because the pressure is so great, be prepared to apologise later if a chance becomes available.

Ultimately, after several warnings, you have to be clear that individual pupils who stop you teaching, by persistently breaking the rules, will be punished or removed from the room. If you are clear that there is a limit, many pupils will back down. Most pupils want the teacher to establish clear limits so that they can learn. But you can tell the pupil that this is not what you want. You want to give them a way out. If you can give the rest of the class a task to get on with while you handle the most obstinate pupil, this will help keep the momentum of your lesson and increase your authority with the group. Your school should have a behaviour man-agement system, where senior staff are on call to support you in this approach. You need to show that you will take charge where you can but sending a child to fetch a colleague, when you really have to, should not be seen as a sign of weakness, rather a sign of the teachers working together. Those teachers who feel they cannot share their difficulties do not aid good behaviour patterns across the school.

Worst case scenarios

In the very worst scenario, you may not get silence when you want to introduce your lesson because a large group of children refuse to listen. Do not be surprised by this; although schools are reluctant to admit it, many other staff with challenging groups will be experiencing similar problems. You should always try to have an introductory activity ready and use a cueing system; these two tactics will give you the best chance of a positive response. However, even with these approaches, the moment for listening may be very brief and you may have to make a very hasty introduction and circulate around the room to explain the task more thoroughly. It may even be necessary to explain the task to the students who are willing to work and then tackle the others. These pupils sometimes change their mind about being willing to work when they are getting less attention for misbehaviour. Alternatively, stop talking, write a cloze on the board and see who will cooperate from there. You are trying to maximise the numbers who cooperate with these strategies.

To get the lesson started when there is a large group of students refusing to cooperate is a highly stressful and difficult moment which many teachers experience regularly in challenging schools. The great irony of inner-city schools full of loud, uncooperative adolescents is that new teachers, even new but experienced teachers, have to go through an initiation process, a baptism of fire or trial by ordeal, to prove themselves. You have to have a variety of responses to overcome the situation or the pupils will take complete control and nothing will be achieved. Continuing to speak while pupils persistently interrupt is a mistake, but just waiting for silence can also get you nowhere. You can end up waiting for a whole lesson. You have to show that, whatever happens, the pupils are going to learn with you. Tell them they are going to learn with you despite their misbehaviour.

What you are trying to communicate in this situation is that your spirit is indomitable, even if you have been ignored for part of the lesson. The more you get them to work, the more they will be prepared to listen and eventually accept your instructions for the lessons that follow. What you are really doing is building up a relationship with them despite their resistance. What they come to admire is your persistence. It should be remembered that the reason many of these children are contemptuous of adults is because other adults have given up on them so often. Some children from socially disadvantaged backgrounds have been left to grow up without adequate adult guidance. Society has let them down time and time again. It therefore takes time and persistence for any adult to win the trust of these children. Teachers cannot compensate overnight for all the ills of society.

Making the most of your body language and voice

Children, of all ages, are very shrewd. They can tell from your body language, even before you open your mouth, what kind of teacher you are. Between 70 and 90 per cent of all communication is non-verbal. How you stand, your eye contact, how you move around the room, the way you hold yourself, what you do with your hands and possessions – these are all vital factors influencing the pupils' judgement of the teacher. There are a lucky few teachers who rarely need to work at establishing their authority. The overwhelming majority of teachers, however, are not like that. They have to work extremely hard at establishing authority – particularly in the most challenging schools.

How to stay relaxed

This is why staying relaxed is often the key feature of good teacher talk and control. Whatever your personality, size and appearance you must show the pupils that you are comfortable with who you are. Do not try to emulate the barking deputy head. Cheeky adolescents will pick on your appearance, mannerisms, speech and possessions to try to undermine you. As suggested earlier, try deliberately ignoring some silly behaviour. Your self-confidence is the greatest weapon you have. Initially, when addressing the class, stand in a relaxed posture, make eye contact with different students as you speak. When the pupils are working or you are reading, circulate around the room. Join the pupils in the group work when appropriate. Sit down and read from the front, then move around and sit down again at the back of the room. Make sure you send out the message that this is your domain. If you can keep your head, your poise, your self-confidence . . . you will generally manage to gain and keep the attention of most of your pupils, most of the time.

Some female teachers find that their voice goes up a level when they are dealing with a large degree of non-cooperation. This can open the door to loud mimicry and abuse. It is therefore a good idea to use pauses and stop speaking if you feel your voice rising. When you do speak again try to keep your voice at an even level, or lower, and quieten it when you feel annoyed. If you can be conscious about your voice and stay as relaxed as possible, you will be more effective.

Make sure they know you are human

Try to remember that much of misbehaviour is playful. However, when you feel really ground down by misbehaviour and it seems that no one is listening, it's a good idea to release your feelings in some way. You cannot hold yourself responsible for all the wild forms of behaviour that you may be confronted with. If you have prepared your lesson you have done the maximum. If you can find something funny to say, this will show the pupils that you are a human being. Tell them how you are feeling but make it into a joke. The more motivated children will listen to this and it helps them to understand some of your dilemmas. Just for a surprise, take a deep breath and allow a long sigh of despair to escape from your mouth. This gives you the chance to articulate your frustration and usually causes the pupils to laugh. For a fleeting moment they may notice you are human and then you can get them back to work. Avoid telling them that they are the worst class you have ever taught. Children enjoy your ranting but you soon realise that it is not having the desired effect. Much better to say that you are disappointed with them today because . . . and you know they can do better. Ultimately, it is the relationship you are building that wins the class round, not your power and authority.

Allow time for informal talk between pupils and teachers

Sometimes children hang back in class because they want some one-to-one conversation or clarification. Sometimes teachers and pupils exchange information and anecdotes in lessons that are nothing to do with the lesson topic. In the playground the chats you have often give you valuable insights into your students. The teacher who is open to this kind of talk will win more trust from the pupils and that teacher will earn more respect.

Reading a class text

Pre-reading

Before you read aloud, think about the genre, themes, characters, setting and events of the story or text and how you can introduce the pupils to this text. Many of the pupils in inner-city schools will struggle with the language of the text and have difficulties understanding the narrative because their literacy levels are below average. There are 10, 11, 12, 13 year olds sitting before you but their reading ages can be 3 or 4 years below their actual age.

Before starting to read you need to get the pupils ready to read. Your task here is to get the pupils fascinated by the text before they even read it. Get them in a state of excitement, of wanting more and understanding some of what the text is about even before they look at it. Here are a few suggestions:

- Deconstruct the book cover with questions about genre, audience, character, themes, setting.
- Find other pictures, a poem or a news story that allows the pupils to gain more knowledge of the book.
- When reading a play about truancy discuss what we mean by truancy, and why pupils truant, before you start to read the play.
- Before you start on a non-fiction text try to find an activity that will introduce them to the style of the text. If you are going to write recipes, stand at the front and pretend that you are Delia Smith or Jamie Oliver or show an appropriate TV clip. They will be far more interested in recipes after that.
- Read the first paragraph and get the pupils to annotate, making comments about characters, settings, themes or language use or just read silently. Silent moments are important for reflective reading/thinking.
- Choose a particularly dramatic moment in a story or play and read this part first as an introduction. Use this to discuss characters and settings and to predict events and themes.
- Choose some more challenging words that are going to come up in the text and get children to look them up in dictionaries or word history books.

The moving image

Television is the currency of the young. The visual and aural literacy of all pupils can be used as a stimulus for reading even very challenging texts. Using their media knowledge will boost their confidence and aid them in analysing written texts. The interactive whiteboard has brought the big screen into the classroom. Successful teachers in challenging contexts will want to take advantage of this. For example:

- Read the first page of any text and ask the children to think/write what they remember and/or design a storyboard for a film version. Watch the film and compare the director's ideas with their own. Then read on. For more ideas on working with film adaptations, see Grahame (1991).

- Watch the first part of a film. Brainstorm some key words. Get the pupils to write a paragraph and then read the first page of the book and compare their version with the author's.
- Watch the first part of the film with groups focusing on different aspects, e.g. the use of the *camera* and type of shots; the use of *colour*, considering colours used and differences if filmed in black and white; the *characters* we meet, what they are wearing, how they behave; the *storyline*; the different *sounds*; and the *setting*, as suggested by the BFI (2001). This can lead into a discussion about different devices used by a film director and an author. Then read the passage and ask the pupils to make some comparisons between the film and the text.
- Freeze-frame a key moment in the film and ask pupils to make a mise en scene analysis, describing everything they can see in the frame, how characters and objects are placed, how lighting is used, as suggested by the BFI (2003).
- Cover the screen for the first few minutes and ask the children to make notes on the sounds they hear and ask them to make predictions about the setting.

All these pre-reading activities are pupil centred and will involve pupil talk and develop reader response.

Organising the reading

When it comes to reading aloud, think carefully about how the text will be read and your aims in choosing that method of reading. One of the main reasons you need to read the text as a class, in challenging classrooms, is that many pupils in the room will find it difficult to read a challenging text independently.

Here are some strategies and routines for organising the reading:

- Give less able readers a summary or an abridged version to read on their own at home so that they can keep up with the story, re-reading if necessary.
- Make sure you summarise or check that the narrative is understood before reading on.

- For less able readers it is a good idea to have key words or questions written down in order, in advance, to assist them in keeping track of the text. For younger children and pupils very new to English, you might use pictures or get them to draw pictures.

Tell the pupils how you will involve them in the reading. There are endless ways you can vary the reading process in the classroom, even when reading as a class together.

- The pupils may be just listening and following or they may be more directly involved.
- Make sure the pupils are reminded of the order of the reading, if they are participating, by writing their names down.
- For a play, the roles should be allocated before you start each scene.
- For a poem, you might want to read alternate lines or verses with one or more pupils.
- For a non-fiction text, get the pupils to identify titles, sub-headings, diagrams, pictures and captions before reading.
- Make sure you are aware of the different reading abilities. By asking for volunteers you can usually select the pupils who are the most confident readers.
- Dramatic readings by the pupils in groups will lead to greater involvement, which is discussed in Chapter 6.

The teacher reading aloud

Reading should be a pleasurable activity for the pupils and the teacher. The teacher's role is to ensure that the pupils engage with the text being read to make their own meaning. Techniques for engaging the class as you read might include:

- a focus on the dialogue: as you read the text, you can emphasise the dialogue by adopting different voices or asking a volunteer to read with you. Pupils enjoy hearing the teacher or other pupils adopting different voices.
- a focus on dialect: when reading poems like 'Wha fe Call I' by Valerie Bloom or 'Half-Caste' by John Agard the teacher can attempt a Jamaican or Trinidadian accent. A pupil can then be invited to improve on this. In a multicultural classroom the pupils warm to this approach, which celebrates the rich variety of language use.

- Reading non-fiction texts aloud can also be made enjoyable by adopting different voices and giving a persona to the writer.
- A change of pace: dramatic moments in writing that call for shorter sentences can be emphasised during the reading by intonation and pace and then discussed by the class.
- Poetry and drama lend themselves to dramatic and cooperative readings.
- Reading pupils' stories and texts aloud can also assist them in becoming more self-critical and more aware of the skills involved in speech and writing.

Remember, you do not always have to 'study' a text and deconstruct it, you can just read it with the pupils if you organise the reading in the right way. In doing this you are teaching the pupils that reading is a pleasure in itself.

Questions

Young children continually ask questions of their parents. As children get older the teacher in school takes over the role of questioner and asks many questions of the children, who are consequently less likely to ask questions as they grow up. However, their natural curiosity is still there. The teacher needs to be a skilful questioner, in all phases of schooling, to create an ethos that fosters enquiry and the sharing of knowledge.

Planning questions

Teachers should plan their questions as the right questions will boost pupil response. To aid your planning you might:

- have a key question written below the learning outcomes as a focus for the pupils' thinking and to allow them time to prepare a response.
- think about differentiated questioning. You often need an 'either/ or' question to include the less able child. You need closed questions to check basic learning and you need open questions to extend children's thinking, to allow them to express preferences and develop their imagination.

  Some suggestions for more open questions might be:

Who do you think this text is written for?

What do you think the author is trying to tell us?

Which part of the text did you enjoy reading? Why?

Which character do you identify with most?

What do you think will happen next? What made you think that?

What obstacles did you have to overcome to produce that?

What was in the character's mind when they said . . .?

What if a different character had joined the conversation there?

Can you say that in a different way?

What would be the point of view of someone who disagreed?

If you could ask the author a question, what would it be?

- display some of these questions on the wall or have a question of the week to encourage pupils to value question time.
- model questions by writing out the stem of an answer or model the answer 'I think this because . . .' or 'On the one hand' and 'On the other hand . . .'.
- prompt pupils by asking 'Why or how do they know that?' or 'Tell me more about . . .'.
- scaffold their thinking by, for example, playing devil's advocate, something that they can usually spot quickly and thoroughly enjoy.
- peer scaffold questions by asking pupils to think up questions in pairs and groups to ask each other.
- vary the pace and challenge of questions in other ways, e.g. 'Hands up all those who have seen . . .' Get a response from a large number. Go for a direct, concentrated response from one pupil and you will get everyone listening. Give one pupil six questions in a row and see how dramatic the effect can be.
- allow pupils to 'phone a friend' for help if they need it, as in the TV game show 'Who Wants to be a Millionaire?'
- train yourself to give pupils thinking time. You can allow pupils a waiting time of 3–5 seconds to allow both teacher and pupils to prepare more thoughtful answers. You can also extend this into thinking time of 30–60 seconds before expecting students to answer or allowing partner talk on other occasions.
- encourage pupils to take the lead in questioning. You can give them structures for this, e.g. a key word such as 'Who . . .' to begin the question, or some examples. If they are then given time to prepare questions at the beginning and told they will be asking them at the end, they will be clear that the activity has a purpose. When you have a character in the hot-seat, questions get thought up quite quickly.

- plan for off-the-cuff questions by creating a slot in the lesson where pupils ask the teacher. You can be in a particular role or just the teacher for this.

Higher-order skills

Bloom's taxonomy, originally devised in 1952, has focused teacher attention on higher-order skills in questioning to encourage pupils to synthesise, evaluate, speculate and hypothesise (see Figure 2.1).

A good way of structuring this approach to questions can be to look at a problem from different angles. When reading a book, choose a theme, e.g. flying in the Harry Potter series. Turn it into a question: 'What if we could fly?' Then ask pupils to draw three columns, one for good points, one for bad points and a third for interesting points. The response can result in a discussion for a whole hour as pupils speculate on traffic jams in the sky and new kinds of transport and maps. Use of the moving image can also act as a stimulus to allow pupils to compare, predict and express empathy as we have already noted.

Sharing knowledge

There must always be room for spontaneity in questioning and response from the teacher. A teacher does have to plan but he or she also has to

---

Comprehension

Name, state, describe, where, what

Application

How, why, illustrate, summarise, use, predict, show me where

Analysis

Break this down into: relate this to, compare this with

Synthesis

Design, create, compose, reorganise

Evaluation

Assess, evaluate, justify

Figure 2.1 Bloom's taxonomy.

think off the top of their head and be able to respond to the real meaning behind an answer in order to unlock the pupils' thought process and build on this.

Once you create an ethos where questions can come from pupils and teachers, and that all answers have some kind of validity and can help in the learning process, everyone will be happier in responding to challenges. The teacher also becomes more willing to show children that they are also learners and have strategies for finding out if they do not immediately know the answer.

In difficult classrooms teachers find themselves repeating answers because pupils are talking over other pupils or over the teacher. By using good cueing systems, using an effective stimulus, modelling good questions and answers, preparing pupils to ask and answer questions and creating clear moments and rules for the class discussion, you can maximise your success. These strategies can lead to effective teacher talk and purposeful question-and-answer sessions – a learning dialogue where knowledge is shared.

Key points: Teacher talk

- Be prepared for the pupils with a calmer and use praise
- Cue the pupils to listen to you and teach them how to listen
- Think about your audience when you talk or read aloud
- Use students' prior knowledge, visual and aural literacy
- Plan a key question and a range of questions
- Allow thinking time when appropriate
- Teach the pupils to ask and to answer questions
- Try to relax and be positive.

Chapter 3

Paired talk

> Language in the classroom should be an instrument of learning not of teaching.
>
> Britton (cited in Jones, 1988)

There are many paired talk tasks that can enhance understanding and pupil engagement in your lessons. Having a large repertoire of smaller talk tasks at your fingertips will make you a versatile and adaptable teacher and ensure that good learning takes place in your lessons. It will mean that you can plan lessons adjusted to the needs of your audience – the pupils – and that they will gain more confidence as learners. You will always be able to think of something to do if you finish early and you will find that you can quickly adapt a cover lesson that has been very formally planned – where, for example, the pupils have been asked to draw a diagram and make notes – by adding a talk task to make it more fun for the pupils.

The best way to introduce such exercises is by getting pupils to work in pairs for a short period at first. All classroom layouts make this possible and there is little movement involved. It is assumed that you have settled the class in the manner suggested in Chapter 2, or using your own methods, before you begin to explain these exercises. If you wish to model the exercise, by showing the pupils how to sit and look at the person they are talking to, before the class attempts it, this may help the pupils understand what you require them to do. A good way to start with this type of exercise is to choose your most responsive group and plan for morning sessions. In this way you can experiment with these strategies in the best conditions.

Over a period of time both you and the pupils will feel more comfortable with these exercises and you will hopefully find that you feel more relaxed with your class and that your lessons work better. You may then decide to move onto more challenging talk tasks. This chapter starts with some of the simplest ideas for small talk tasks and moves onto slightly more complex ones.

Talk partners

This is a vital technique in training pupils to think, articulate, share and deepen knowledge. The pupils are asked to turn to their talk partner and for two minutes to:

- brainstorm an idea
- read all or part of their story, poem or text to their partner
- explain the task for the lesson to their partner
- explain a new word using their own language
- recall an experience in their own life that links to an event in a story, e.g. feeling unfairly treated
- make a list
- turn a non-fiction text into a flow chart
- draw a mind map for . . .
- annotate a text with drawings or words
- rank the statements
- compare two things
- recount an event or experience
- consider the pros and cons
- put some statements or thoughts into different columns such as positive, negative, unsure
- look at an incomplete text where they have to predict the ending
- rewrite a short text for a different audience
- summarise another text.

This paired talk exercise can be used at any point in a lesson. Make sure every pupil knows who they are working with. As you develop more confidence you might want to structure the exercise with a talk frame (see Figure 3.1), some kind of diagram or chart to assist the discussion. The pupils become accountable as they report back to the class.

A slight adaptation of this exercise is 'think, pair, share' where the pupils are asked to think about the topic, talk to their partner and then share their ideas with the whole group.

Should school uniform be abolished?

Arguments for	Arguments against
•	•
•	•
•	•

Figure 3.1 Example of a talk frame.

Keeping everyone on task

The potential problems of such paired exercises are that some pupils talk off task or refuse to work with their partner. Walk around the room to monitor what the children are doing. In the former case, you will need to work with the pair that is off task to demonstrate. If there are a larger number off task, you will realise that the exercise is unclear and that the task needs to be demonstrated again or clarified in some way. Use those pupils who have grasped the idea to demonstrate the task for you to make the second explanation more interesting. Pupils often listen more closely to each other than they do to you. If a child refuses to work with another pupil try cajoling or, quietly, change pupils around. You want to try to educate pupils in the view that they can work with anyone, but sometimes you will need to make concessions in order to maintain the momentum in your lessons.

Visualisation

A simple technique for stopping the lesson and getting the pupils to think more carefully about something and to increase their ability to talk on a topic is 'visualisation'. You ask the children to turn a television screen on in their heads and just imagine the scene, event, person or object as if it were on a TV screen in front of them. Moments for reflection are very valuable in lessons. Like silent reading, this activity changes the mood in the classroom by encouraging silent thought and adding variety to lessons. If the pupils are not always sure what they will be asked to do next by their teacher, then they will be more expectant and therefore listen more attentively. After visualising their scene, they can describe it to their partner or the class.

Keeping everyone on task

A problem might occur with children not taking the exercise seriously. You can warn that child that they will be chosen to explain their TV screen. This usually reminds the child that they will gain more teacher attention from completing the task rather than trying to undermine it.

Twos–Fours

If you want to move the discussion on from talk partners, you may ask a pair to link up with another pair to become a four:

- An example of working in fours is a pupil might be asked, when reading a text, to choose a character and describe themselves as that character to their partner. The partner repeats the activity for another character. The two characters then introduce each other to another pair. This group of four then becomes a panel of four characters ready, for example, to discuss a particular event or issue in the story. To assist this you may wish to produce character cards for the pupils.
- Another example could involve breaking up a text into sections and giving two different sections to different pairs. When they come together they have to explain their section to the other pair.

These activities give a real purpose and context for talk, checking comprehension, encouraging personal response to literature and developing listening and speaking skills.

Keeping everyone on task

In order to have a discussion, pupils must have something to list, add, change, rank or give new information about. If the quality of the exercise is good it will engage the pupils, so always ask yourself 'Will this activity lead to a real discussion?' when setting up such an exercise. Any problems of off task behaviour can be addressed as for talk partners. Don't worry about stopping a discussion and bringing them back to you. Use an appropriate cue system as outlined in the previous chapter.

Snowballing

Pupils are asked to think on their own about a topic or an idea. An example might be how to improve school meals, always a hot topic. They then work through the following stages:

- Each student compiles a short list of, say, two suggestions.
- They *compare* their list with that of their partner. They discuss which points they want to add on a common list of, say, six points.
- Each pair now joins up with another pair; they narrow down their points to four key areas, put them in order and give reasons for each one. This latter activity requires clear *decision-making* and *reasoning*.

Keeping everyone on task

This exercise will work best if pupils are familiar with talking in pairs, but it is also important that the teacher interrogates the exercise to ensure that each stage presents a new challenge and builds on the previous stage, starting with *recall*, moving to *comparison* and finally to a *decision-making* stage, which can fruitfully involve four pupils.

An extension of this exercise is to start in twos, move to fours and then into eights, but only when you and the pupils are ready for this. Seating arrangements will also have to be thought through and the teacher will need to make it very clear to the pupils who they will be working with at each stage.

Interviews in role

A way of giving partner work more stimulus is by asking pupils to assume a role as they interview each other. The possibilities are endless here:

- A TV presenter interviewing a famous or less famous personality.
- A newspaper reporter of that period collecting information about, for example, the slave trade.
- A child from the school council interviewing a librarian about a book for the school newspaper.
- A reporter, or another character, interviewing a character in a story, play, poem or news report.

You may wish to establish the framework by writing the beginning of the script down and modelling it with one pupil working with you in front of the class, to get the pupils started. Some pupils who are new to English can work with a support teacher to model the language required.

Keeping everyone on task

Children who have been absent from school may lack knowledge of the characters involved. In this case your introduction can revise the text to assist these children and the rest of the class in being ready for the exercise. Remember that many pupils, particularly pupils with lower reading ages, need help with recalling the narrative for activities such as this.

Back to back

Another way of creating dialogue is to ask pupils to sit back to back and write down what they are saying to each other. For example, a parent does not want his son or daughter to date this particular friend. The teacher establishes the scenario. The argument begins. The parent is adamant; the child argues back; the parent wins out in the end. Ask the pupils to write out what each character says and hand the paper back to their partner as if they are playing consequences. The teacher can then allow some of the pupils to read the script aloud or read it herself. The use of such themes can be used to highlight the central storylines of texts, such as *Romeo and Juliet*.

This is a very useful approach with turbulent groups as the discipline of writing in this way, using realistic dialogue, is accessible and fun. It is speechless conversation. The final product is obviously amusing when read out aloud and pupils enjoy performing their short plays.

Keeping everyone on task

The pupils will often be using colloquial language in this exercise and most of them will be able to write out the conversation. However, look out for pupils who may need some help with key words and even those who may need you to scribe for them.

Radio plays

Any story, or part of a story, can be turned into a radio script and recorded as a play. This is not necessarily a medium the pupils are that familiar with and you may wish to tape an example for them. They will, however, be familiar with music stations and quickly understand and enjoy inventing sound effects, if the teacher points them in the right direction. Pupils love hearing their voices on tape and enjoy using tape recorders or dictaphones. This activity not only involves using multisensory skills, but is very popular with pupils and is excellent as an extension exercise in both primary and secondary schools.

Keeping everyone on task

The plays can be written during a whole-class session but need to be recorded group by group. You need to find a safe and quiet venue for this: a library or a classroom where the pupils are unlikely to be interrupted. The exercise provides a good opportunity to encourage a support teacher to supervise. The outcome is clear and the adult can ensure that the pupils are focused and that others do not interrupt them.

Questions to each other

As suggested in the previous chapter, at any point in the lesson pupils can be told that they are going to devise questions on the subject of the lesson to ask each other at the end. You can give a structure for these questions by using the six 'W's:

- Who?
- What?
- Where?
- When?
- Why?
- What if?

Or just give them some examples to follow.

For younger primary pupils and some of those pupils new to English in secondary schools, it may be necessary to plant questions or the beginnings of questions. The pupils can move into fours to ask and answer questions. Or the plenary can become a session that the pupils lead. If you want to give an edge to this exercise ask the pupils to name someone in the class to answer the question. If this pupil gets it right then they name another pupil to answer their questions. This has an electric effect on the class and focuses the minds of all those listening.

Keeping everyone on task

Working in groups to ask and answer questions will allow all children to participate fully in the final exercise. Organising pupil question-and-answer sessions can involve the teacher or the pupils choosing the person who answers.

While pupils choosing those who have to answer is highly interactive and brings in an element of challenge, it is a good idea to introduce the device of 'phone a friend' before you start in order to lessen the competitive element in the exercise. The game atmosphere, your sensitive approach and explanation that this particular exercise is simply a device to ensure that everyone listens and learns together should make this experience enjoyable for all. You may wish to record individual pupil evaluations to get feedback on such exercises. This is discussed in more detail in Chapter 9.

Quizzes

A quiz can always be used successfully to check that learning is effective. There are many ways of planning a quiz:

- The teacher prepares a series of questions in advance on a relevant topic and the students work out the answers, often in pairs, on the prepared sheet or whiteboard. The teacher can then mark or check them orally in class.
- The teacher may choose to present the quiz as multiple-choice or as a true/false exercise.
- The teacher can read out the questions; the pupils write down the answers. Then you check them orally and put up the names of those who answer correctly.
- A group quiz can be based on a chapter of a book, the complete

book or any aspect of knowledge you may choose. The following stages will ensure a successful group quiz:

1   The teacher chooses the groups with the aim of creating mixed ability groups.
2   The teacher gives each group a named leader and ten listening points for each group. Points will be deducted for any unnecessary interruptions.
3   The groups are named Group 1, 2, 3, 4, 5, etc.
4   Group 1 asks Group 2 a question. If the answer is correct Group 2 gets two points. If the question has to be asked again to another group, this second group gets one point. If nobody in the class can answer the question correctly the original group gains one point.
5   The teacher explains that the groups gain two points for correctly answering another group's question the first time. A group gains one point if no one but them can answer it.
6   The teacher also reminds the class that she may add a difficult question that will be worth more points at the end.
7   Group 1 asks Group 2 a question and so on until all groups have completed the exercise. The teacher must ensure that one or two full rounds are played so that each group has the same chances of scoring.
8   The teacher then counts up the scores for each group and announces the winning team.
9   The teacher may generate the questions but it is more challenging and interesting when the pupils themselves devise the questions.

Keeping everyone on task

Group quizzes or those in which children work in pairs are more participatory than individual quizzes. However, if you allow the students to mark their own answers in the lesson this gives them instant feedback, allowing them to find out what they know and what they need to know. Listening marks, a tally of ten to begin, keep pupils from shouting out and lend more order to these sessions.

The teacher must plan for rewards for these quizzes. The whole class can be rewarded with a merit or other small reward if the quiz has gone well, while groups that have shown exceptional skill or made particularly good progress can be awarded certificates. If you want students to a put a special effort into a classroom event, you must plan for a special reward. Edible prizes can be purchased at the end of term. It is a sad fact that in very challenging classrooms, those who turn up for the last day are often the most motivated students and they will particularly enjoy having fun with an intellectual challenge in your end-of-term lessons. Quizzes are often preferred to videos/DVDs as a treat.

Show and tell or individual talks

In primary schools children are often asked to bring something into the class from home and show the picture or object to the class, talk about why they have chosen it and take questions from the group. This simple technique can be used in a variety of ways with pupils of any age. They can be asked to:

- tell jokes in a joke session
- bring poems to read aloud or music to play
- talk about their favourite book, author, TV programme, painting or advert
- prepare the case for . . . or the case against . . .
- prepare a talk on a subject of their choice
- give an off-the-cuff talk on a topic chosen by an individual, the class or the teacher. (This is more challenging and should only be used when you feel the children are ready for it.)

Pupils can talk first to a partner or group and then talk in front of the class if they wish to. The teacher can give pupils advice about the form or content of talks and presentations where they think it is appropriate, e.g. how to use visual aids or artefacts. The pupils bring their own tastes and lifestyles into the classroom through these exercises and some of the barriers between home and school are broken down. Multicultural differences can often be celebrated in this context.

The pupils of all ages are very keen to learn more about their teacher. On many talk topics it may be possible for the teacher to introduce the lesson by giving their own talk on that topic. This is real talk from the teacher and shows that the teacher wants to make connections with the pupils but it also models the exercise for the pupils. The result is that the pupils are usually fully engaged. When teachers tell stories, jokes or personal anecdotes the class tends to be at its most attentive. A good narrative or a human-interest story engages even the toughest pupils.

Chapter 5 gives more advice on how a teacher can develop their story-telling techniques.

Keeping everyone on task

For individual talks it is often preferable for such exercises to take place first in pairs or groups. This gives a more informal structure for the pupils to practise the exercise. Girls will often be more likely to contribute in this structure. Pupils can then volunteer to speak to the class if they wish to, having fine-tuned their speech a little. This structure also allows the teacher to check that the talk is appropriate and that it will be well received before the child stands up.

Spread the talks out carefully so that all talks are listened to. You may wish to prepare some kind of listening grid to fill in some details as the individual pupil delivers their talk. However, if the audience is captivated and listening closely this may not be necessary. You have to make this assessment and ensure that all the pupils who wish to talk are listened to.

You do not have to insist on all children presenting their talks, and it may be insensitive to do so, but a number of children will want to and this will make for some interesting lessons. For some EAL pupils, new to English, the listening or practice in the group will be quite stimulating enough.

Some word games

There are vast arrays of word games that you may wish to use to motivate pupils and check learning in your classroom. All children enjoy these exercises but male pupils seem to be particularly engaged by them. Some of these games require only a little preparation and are highly adaptable and therefore of enormous use to a busy teacher. Here are some examples:

- Word tennis: two people face each other and say words from a given category, e.g. makes of cars. They continue until one person has run out of words or repeats a word already used.
- Yes/no: pupils ask each other questions and try to answer without saying 'yes' or 'no'.
- Minister's cat/adjective game: each member of the class repeats in turn that the Minister's cat is a _____ cat. The pupils have to put an adjective in the space using each letter of the alphabet.

- What are they doing adverb game: pupils are asked to mime an action, e.g. sitting or running, in the style of the adverb. The other pupils have to guess the adverb.
- Mime the rhyme: pupils are sent out of the room to think of a word and another word that rhymes with it. The pupils return and mime the word that rhymes with the first word. Then the class has to guess the original word.
- Hang person: this allows pupils to check vocabulary and spelling for any topic you are studying. Pitting the class against the teacher, award points for the class when they win and points for the teacher when the pupils cannot get the word.
- Hobbies: each pupil concentrates on the initials of their name and makes up an imaginary hobby with these letters:

Francis Tilbury – fantastic tennis
Donna Smith – drawing snakes

Play this quickly until only a few are left.

- Chinese whispers: a message is whispered from one pupil to another round the class. No repetition is allowed. Compare the original message with the final one. They usually differ.
- 0 and Xs: this requires two teams. Split the class in half and choose one pupil as the captain of the 0s and another as the captain of the Xs. They choose where the 0 or X goes. You then write six words or short statements on the board and the pupils have to do one of the following:

1   Read the word correctly
2   Make up a sentence using that word
3   Explain a word or concept
4   Give a similar word
5   Identify who said it
6   Find a quote or evidence to back up a point.

Each team is given a chance to answer in turn. The winners are the team that joins up their 0s or their Xs.

- Find words in the word: this is another game that always engages the pupils. A long word like 'Liverpool' can be placed on the board and pupils have to find as many words as they can using the letters of the word.

Keeping everyone on task

Pupils can get very animated and competitive about games. Large team games in particular focus the class on winning. The teacher needs to anticipate this by making the purpose of the game clear – to revise together, to share knowledge – and by rewarding those who play well with verbal and other forms of praise. Most of the time this will be everyone in the classroom.

The teacher needs to develop routines in their teaching that show pupils how to find out things from each other and consolidate learning. In challenging classrooms the pupils often have problems with comprehension. These strategies help pupils to explore a text, sort the trivial from the main ideas in a text, hold the plot in their minds from one lesson to the next and help them to infer hidden meanings. Quizzes and games show pupils that revision and sharing of knowledge can make learning more enjoyable. Regular use of paired talk tasks and language games will lighten the atmosphere in the classroom. These tasks also show how you can teach without having to use too many pieces of paper, too many PowerPoints, and in particular avoid an over-reliance on the comprehension worksheet. You will be less likely to talk *at* the pupils if you use some of these strategies and much more likely to talk *with* them.

Key points: Paired talk

- Pair work allows pupils to clarify ideas and learn from each other
- Pair work helps overcome difficulties with comprehension
- Talk time breaks up a lesson for pupils and teachers and prepares for a more thoughtful discussion
- Clear timing and instructions, even demonstrations, are required
- The teacher should monitor the talk
- Plan to start these exercises with your best group in a morning session.

Chapter 4

Group talk

In group work 'thinking is made explicit'.
Gen Ling Chang and Gordon Wells (1988)

Group work

Group work can be a frightening concept for some teachers. They may see it as an opportunity for pupils to get out of control, talk off task and generally muck about. If the group task does not really require group work this can be the result. The key test for a group task is that the group has to cooperate: the task *must* involve a group decision, negotiation or consensus of some kind, and have a real purpose. This may involve exploring, transforming or preparing to present information. It must be *real* group work if it is to engage the pupils to work together. The group must also be accountable for an outcome. If the task does not involve these skills the group will not truly work as a group.

Why group work helps pupils and teachers

When it works well group work is the most organic form of learning. If students are using their language to make sense of new ideas, learning becomes more effective. Pupils can explore ideas in smaller settings which gives *all* pupils the chance to use the higher-order skills that only the more able or more confident will use in a larger forum. While different inputs are possible, the more able group members scaffold the learning of others as the group moves towards its goals.

For the teacher, group work can overcome many of the problems of dominating discussion and decisions and using too many closed questions. Group work is differentiated because it allows for children to learn from each other, question each other, in a relaxed and familiar context. The teacher can then spend more time listening to students talking and relate to students as individuals more easily. This is an enormous benefit in challenging contexts when some pupils need a lot of one-to-one encouragement to keep focused.

Small group learning can have an enormous impact on pupil self-confidence as the pupils realise that both their own experience and their existing knowledge are valuable in assimilating new ideas. Group work thus changes and improves relationships in the classroom and helps pupils to understand that learning is a collaborative process.

An overall climate for group work

Readers are reminded, as suggested at the very beginning of this book, that there needs to be an appropriate climate for group work to flourish:

- Teachers need to show that they value the pupils' language and comments and that their classroom is a place where small group talk is encouraged.
- Learning aims need to include speaking and listening skills as outcomes.
- The teacher should be prepared to use space creatively to allow for small group work and drama, moving to other rooms if necessary.
- The teacher needs to allow enough time for groups to finish the tasks without prolonging the exercise. Sometimes time limits can focus group work quite effectively; at other times the teacher will need to revise their initial timings.
- The outcomes of small group work need to be made public in some form via display, recording, sharing in new groups, whole class sharing or shown to wider audiences. These outcomes need to be celebrated and praised.

Managing group work: the role of the teacher

The role of the teacher is less obvious in small group work but nevertheless the teacher is scaffolding the learning experience very carefully and therefore the planning and thought required before the lesson is greater. However, the skills and knowledge that the teacher gains from planning in this way will make their future life in the classroom, even in challenging settings, much more successful and enjoyable.

Some issues to think about in planning include:

- A teacher's planning for talk should build on pupils' knowledge and experience. The five-stage model of learning in which students engage, can explore new knowledge, transform, present and reflect (see table on p. 5) helps teachers to do this when planning for learning in small groups. Chapter 11 offers more specific guidance on this.
- You need to know your class as individuals to plan effectively for this kind of work.
- The pupils need a task that is clear and relevant and has a purpose. It should be real group work, i.e. a task that involves comparing, choosing, solving and coming to a consensus. Instructions need to be very specific.
- Key words can help promote thinking before group work takes place to ensure that all pupils can have an input in challenging groups with low reading ages.
- Roles, such as chair, scribe, time-keeper, reporter may be ascribed by the teacher at first to teach children how to work in groups. Dominant children can be asked to chair or scribe to encourage them to allow others to speak more. Particularly disruptive groups can be allowed to work together and praised when they work well. As pupils become more familiar with this model of working, however, the group will work better if they choose their own roles.
- Through reflection at the end of group work all pupils become more aware of how to learn in small groups. This is discussed in more detail in Chapter 9.

As in Chapter 4, it is suggested that you try these tasks out on your best class in the morning first and that you are always ready to prompt groups or pupils who may need more support.

Once again this chapter starts with group tasks with a lighter touch, such as using diagrams to promote group discussion – because drawing is very accessible and it has a calming effect on pupils – and then moves onto group discussion to argue, order, justify or explain. The chapter concludes with a more sustained example of group work using the jigsaw technique. Every example described here has worked successfully in very challenging classrooms.

Lighter touch group work

Group brainstorm or thought shower

Age range: 8–16+; group size: 3–4

Activity: This is a method of generating ideas and beginning a discussion. It can simply be word association or a more directed brainstorm or shower of ideas. A key word is placed in the middle of a large sheet of paper. The large piece of paper and large pens help to involve more pupils and create the group. Pupils are given marker pens to create a diagram of words or symbols they associate with the key word. To develop the brainstorm further pupils could be asked to classify their list into particular categories.

Example: After being given one suggestion by the teacher, pupils might be asked to list the key characters in the novel they are reading, for example *Of Mice and Men* (see Figure 4.1) and then categorise them into major and minor characters. Feedback might involve one group listing characters, other groups adding any missed names. Another group could list minor characters and other group members could interrogate this list, discussing *why* particular characters are placed in the different categories.

Keeping everyone on task

Demonstrate with one or two ideas so that all are clear about the task. Divide pupils into groups and ensure they are sitting so that they can discuss. Circulate around the groups and give praise to groups who are sitting and discussing well to model what you want from others. You can even freeze-frame the group that is working well to demonstrate to others what you want. Time the exercise, collect in the pens, counting them out and in, as magic markers are popular for graffiti. Allow time for discussion during responses.

Group sociogram

Age range: 8–16+ with appropriate texts; group size: 2–4

Activity: This is another diagram technique that aids pupils in thinking about texts. It is based on the idea of complementary opposites, finding

Of Mice and Men
1st stage

2nd stage

Major characters	Minor characters
George	Whit
Lennie	Boss
Curley	Carlson
Curley's wife	The Rabbit
Candy?	
Slim?	
Crooks?	

Figure 4.1 Brainstorm.

characters in a text that represent two sides of the same coin. The class might need to brainstorm some of the main characters first before deciding which character should be placed opposite the other. The sociogram should be modelled by the teacher and then drawn on a large sheet of paper by the pupils. Once the key contrasting characters have been identified pupils are urged to draw symbols to remind them of that character and find a quote from the text that is typical of their role and personality.

For example, *Romeo and Juliet* is full of complementary opposites. Romeo and Juliet, the fiery Tybalt and the peaceful Benvolio, the Nurse and the Friar, who both aid the young lovers. The diagram based on a cross (see Figure 4.2) gives pupils a framework to analyse their thoughts and the exercise allows pupils to produce different outcomes. The pupils think they are drawing but, in reality, they are engaged in a lot of thinking.

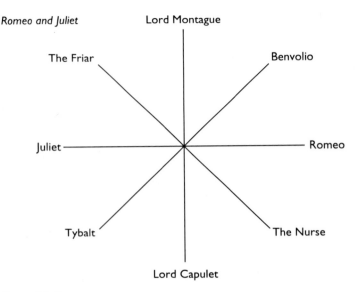

Figure 4.2 Sociogram.

Keeping everyone on task

Some groups may be able to find more than one quote for each character independently while others will need help even to identify the opposites. The teacher needs to be ready to intervene and support groups as necessary. Finding quotations is a skill that may need to be taught or reinforced before the exercise or as a result of the exercise.

Group mind maps

Age range 8–16+ with appropriate texts; group size: 3 or 4

Activity: This is an extension of the brainstorm, used to develop the pupils' thinking skills. Mind maps involve using a diagram to structure thought and to go more deeply into the subject matter. Ideas could be developed from an original stem. The visual structure aids the thought process and once taught the pupils can apply the technique to other subjects and topics.

Example: The teacher places the title *Goodnight Mr Tom* in the middle of the white board and draws four lines coming out from the stem. She asks the class to think of one key event that happened in the story and writes their answer down at the end of one stem as an example (see Figure 4.3). She then asks the pupils to think up some thoughts and questions they would like to ask about that event, discusses these and then asks the question 'What have we learnt about the story from this discussion?' This shows the pupils what she wants them to do and, working in their groups, they carry on choosing three more events which they attempt to analyse in this way.

Groups could then be asked to meet up to check their mind maps or landscapes towards the end of the activity and add to or improve parts of the map. You could ask them what they changed as a result of their discussions and what they might add to a reading log they were writing about this book.

Keeping everyone on task

Pupils enjoy mind-mapping activities as long as they are clearly explained and modelled beforehand. The teacher will need to be ready to intervene to clarify where any confusion arises and repeat explanations. If one group is struggling, the teacher can always work with that group. This is a good idea anyway, to check that the activity is really working to aid the pupils' thinking. Groups will work at different paces but if you give clear and reasonable time limits most groups will get a result that they can share. Counting out the pens and collecting them in before the pupils move into larger groups to share their ideas encourages pupils to respect time limits for the activity and to be ready for the next stage. All diagrams allow the work to be displayed from which the pupils gain a great sense of achievement. Such displays celebrate the process of learning and sharing ideas.

Group discussion to argue, justify, order or explain

Age group: 10–16; group size: 2–4

TABLECLOTH

Activity: This is an excellent method to use in planning any form of discursive writing because it allows pupils to rehearse ideas orally, discussing why a statement is relevant or irrelevant, before starting to write. Coloured A3 pieces of paper are handed to the pupils who are arranged

Plot and structure landscape in *Goodnight Mr Tom*

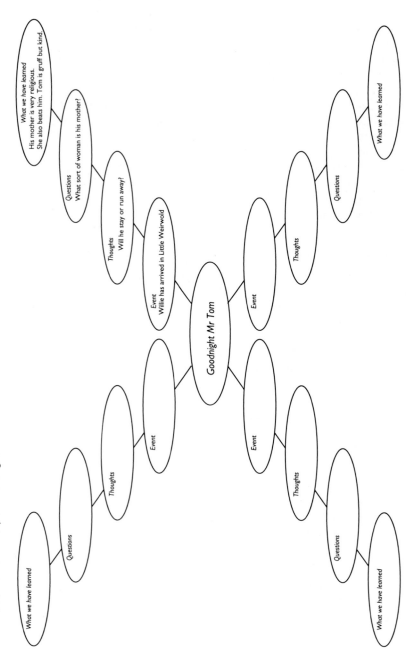

Figure 4.3 Mind mapping.

in groups. A concept or essay title is handed to the groups. Statements on white sheets are handed to the groups to be arranged in different ways. You can ask the pupils to sort the statements into relevant and irrelevant ones, putting the relevant statements on the tablecloth and keeping the irrelevant statements off the cloth. You can then ask pupils to group statements into particular categories.

Example: When studying the Great Fire of London you set the essay title 'Why did the fire get out of control?' A list of statements are given to the pupils, e.g. the houses were made of wood; a hot dry summer led to water supplies being unusually low in 1666; town officials did not believe that it was going to spread and took no action at the start. The pupils then have to group the statements – for example, 'natural causes' or 'human error' – around the title.

Keeping everyone on task

Pupils generally enjoy this kind of activity because it involves moving cards around while they are thinking. The teacher may need to intervene to support the less able directly and/or by stopping the activity and getting pupils to think aloud to prompt others. Take the exercise more slowly and keep prompting if the whole group has low reading ages or if there are a large number of EAL pupils at an early stage of English. Allow time for the collection of your materials so that you do not have to produce them again. Such activities take time to prepare and resources like this are precious.

Group presentations

Age range: 5–18; group size: 3

Activity: This involves asking pupils to give the class some information, in an interesting form, on a topic chosen by the pupils or the teacher. Presentation is business speak for a short, focused talk. It is one of the simplest and most adaptable techniques for involving pupils in the lesson. Pupils can be asked to make a presentation on any subject as a group. The teacher can model, frame or structure a presentation herself. The pupils then prepare their work and present it to the class as a group. You make it clear that everyone in the group must contribute and take a role in the final presentation.

Example: A 'poem poster'. The teacher chooses a poem and models the annotation process, highlighting, for example, words, phrases and images they like and explaining why they find them effective. This shows pupils how to write comments around the poem and draw symbols where appropriate.

Then the pupils are given a large sheet of paper and a poem and they are asked to annotate the poem, highlighting significant words or lines, rhymes, rhythms or repetitions. They are also encouraged to draw pictures to explain feelings or images provoked by the poem. They can add comments of their own or questions to the poet.

They then present their work to the class. To give the pupils more choice you can give them several poems and ask them to choose one to annotate. To develop presentation skills you can ask them to use large pieces of paper, OHTs with marker pens or PowerPoint for this exercise. And, as pupils become more skilled, give them a choice of methods.

In science lessons you can ask pupils to present an evaluation of an experiment. In maths you can ask pupils to report on an investigation. In humanities a case could be argued and in art a picture could be placed on an OHT/PowerPoint and deconstructed. The teacher can provide guidance on the content and the structure of the presentation in their specialist area.

Keeping everyone on task

The role of the audience when listening to a series of presentations can be a problem in challenging schools. The first group is listened to eagerly and then concentration can be lost. There are a number of different ways you can overcome this. First, make your expectations of active listening clear and support this with a grid where pupils record and evaluate each presentation. You may wish to stagger the presentations and have just one or two presentations in each session, if this fits in with your teaching plans. Make sure you keep the materials safely in labelled folders, as the pupils will often fail to do so. Alternatively you may decide that they will present in groups of six to each other or that some groups could visit another class to give their presentation. If they are all annotating the same poem, you might choose to lead a class discussion after one or two presentations so that they can all contribute their thoughts.

Group discussion: choosing or ranking

Age range: 8–16+; group size: 4

Activity: Group discussion and reasoned argument works best when pupils have to make a choice about something or find a solution. They may have to do one of the following: rank statements in order of importance; choose their words to fill in a cloze; decide which is the odd one out; place statements into columns; sequence events in the correct order; predict something; solve a puzzle of some kind or choose a picture to match a character in a story from a number of pictures. It is often useful to ask one child to observe this activity if you are initiating a class into this kind of work. The observer can focus on how well the group works and report back to the class at the end.

Example: A simple one is a survival exercise where the pupils imagine they have been stranded on a desert island and have to choose six out of ten items to help them survive. The objects might include a piece of rope, a tin opener, a flask of ale, a knife, a machete and a conch. The teacher can add some more or less useful objects to the list and add pictures. There are several novels and plays that might inspire this exercise, e.g. *Lord of the Flies, The Tempest, Robinson Crusoe, Kensuke's Kingdom*, or you may just wish to create a scenario to use as a stimulus for creative writing.

Keeping everyone on task

The debate can get very animated because the scenario engages the pupils and they enjoy arguing the case for their item to be kept. The teacher must give clear but reasonable time limits to encourage pupils to come to a final decision and emphasise the need to give clear reasons for their decisions.

Group talk

Age range: 10–16+; group size: 5

Activity: This is a talk given to a group on any subject or topic. Each member of the class prepares the talk in advance and then children take turns to introduce their talk. It may be necessary to have one pupil act as a chair to time the speakers, field questions and ensure everyone has a turn. Pupils can amaze teachers with their choice of topics if you make the choice of topic open-ended. You can often learn more about that pupil from this discussion than at any other moment in their school career if you can sit and listen to these talks. You learn much about the rich cultural backgrounds of the children you teach and their underlying values.

Example: A talk on a book of their choice. The teacher can structure this activity by giving or recording a talk on a book of their choice, possibly one that the pupils might like to read or one that has already had a particular impact on them. The teacher gives the talk and at the end asks the pupils to consider how their attention was held throughout the 5-minute talk. The pupils give their suggestions and the teacher prompts the pupils to focus on features such as:

- how to start, explaining why you chose to talk about this book
- comments on important characters, exciting events and how the writer engages the reader
- the purpose of the talk is to tempt the listeners to read the book, not tell the whole story.

This provides a simple talk framework for the pupils to follow if they need to when preparing their talk at home for the next lesson. The pupils then work in small groups to listen to each other's talks.

The teacher can ask for volunteers to speak to the class at the end or draw out some general features of the books that were selected, using the lesson as a spur to encourage wider reading and private reading for pleasure. The teacher may have a reading wall; each brick representing a book read by a member of the class, and the pupils can add their books to this.

Keeping everyone on task

The teacher will need to have some popular books available or spares of a class novel to support children who have not prepared a talk. A short amount of time will be needed to support these pupils in preparing their talk and allowing others to revise their task. This activity depends on all the children being prepared and in challenging schools positive action is needed to support children who have lower levels of literacy, confidence or less parental back up for homework. It is no good just using punishment; you have to offer support to show these pupils how to overcome obstacles. You need to explain to these pupils that next time they must ask the teacher, the librarian or the support teacher to help them find a book in advance of the lesson. The groups work best when all the children can contribute.

Simulations

Age range: 10–16; group size: 4

Activity: This group activity involves pupils becoming a team or group in a decision-making process. They could be the school council or a governing body deciding to spend a certain amount of money on the school or discussing which candidate, out of several made-up candidates, should be appointed as a new teacher. They could be any group of people in role trying to make a group decision of some kind. The pupils will need to have some familiarity with the roles.

Example: A local radio news team is given a list of 20 items that they could place on their programme at 7 o'clock that evening. The news team has to choose items for a 5-minute slot. They may want to allocate roles such as editor, anchorperson and interviewer. Five minutes will allow them time for about four or five items. You also suggest that they may want a slot for listener responses to a previous news item. They start to discuss their priorities. After 20 minutes you announce that there has been a huge accident on . . . They then have to reassess their priorities. In another lesson you consider theme tunes for radio and TV news stations and get them to consider how they will simulate this with the equipment available. This exercise can be completed with a tape recorder or dictaphone and a simple sound system, or it can be recorded and edited in a radio suite if available. The final outcome is the broadcast on live radio.

Keeping everyone on task

The groups quickly get involved in choosing items. Mixed ability groups are best because of the reading and editing skills involved and the teacher may have to determine the groups to ensure a balanced composition. The desire to get it absolutely perfect leads to requests to re-record and the pupils have to be allowed out of the class into a quiet room to do this. If possible, with younger groups a support teacher or librarian/media resources officer (MRO) could be helpful in assisting the recording process. Older pupils, however, need to experience working as a team, over a period of time, towards a common goal, imposing their own collective self-discipline to complete the exercise. This activity is a very life-like simulation that shows pupils how valuable teamwork is in the real world of work, family and personal life.

Independent research groups

Age range: 8–16+ with appropriate texts; group size: 3/4

Activity: This is a more pupil-centred variant of the guided reading group where the teacher reads or discusses a text with a small group. It is particularly useful for extension activities. It involves the teacher preparing a study pack on a particular topic, placing the sheets in a folder and asking a small group of students to research the topic and produce some teaching materials for the whole class. The librarian can be given a copy of the project so she can assist students if they need help. When this was tried out with students it was such a successful activity that the students demanded that more study packs were prepared so that they could all prepare a mini-lesson for the class. The audience is a direct one and the feedback extremely quick, giving students very clear goals to work towards.

Example: The study of symbolism in *To Kill a Mockingbird*. The pupils are given a pack that contains a mind-mapping exercise, a series of sheets from a Letts Study Guide and some suggestions for exercises that the class might attempt on symbolism. The pupils have two lessons only to study the materials and provide an exercise for the class. The pupils study the materials and prepare a diagram with questions to explain the symbolism of the references to the mockingbird in the text. They explain how the mockingbird stands for innocence and how Tom Robinson, Boo Radley and the children share the characteristics of innocence and harmlessness – yet are also victims, as the mockingbird can be. They prepare the diagram and a few questions and present them to the class. This could stimulate an interesting discussion about, for example, what we mean by a symbol and the term symbolism which leads into a discussion about the different messages and meanings in the text. Classes often enjoy the mini-lesson and are impressed by other students' knowledge. The research group could become a regular treat for different groups.

Keeping everyone on task

The teacher needs to give copies of the exercise to the librarian before-hand to help the pupils if they need any further information. The teacher needs to read and evaluate the pupil's final product, the worksheet, notes or presentation to the class, then type it up as an exercise for other pupils to use in a lesson.

More sustained group work

Jigsaw

Age range: 5–16+ with appropriate texts; group size: 5/6 unless classes smaller than 25

Activity: This is an excellent technique for structuring group work and extending discussion over several lessons. This activity can be used for any topic or text in any subject. It involves breaking up the learning into separate sub-groups or topics so that groups *specialise* in one area and come together to share their expertise in a new context. The jigsaw is completed when the pupils return to their *home* groups. The key point of the Jigsaw is that only one pupil in each home group has the specialist knowledge, which forces groups to share knowledge and encourages everyone to participate.

Example: Casting actors as characters in a play, e.g. *Macbeth*. In the first session the pupils work in specialist groups to interrogate the qualities of a particular character, listing adjectives to describe that character and considering the type of person required to act that role. The pupils move back to their original/home groups (see Figure 4.4) to consider the different characters and the qualities required. The teacher leads a discussion on their findings.

In the second session the pupils stay in their home groups to sift through a selection of large photographs of actors who are 'auditioning' for each of the five or six roles under consideration: Macbeth, Lady Macbeth, Banquo, King Duncan, the Witches, Macduff. They have a set amount of time to make their choice and the group lists clear reasons. After a few minutes the pictures of that character move on to another group and so on, until all the groups have chosen an actor for each part.

For the final session, the pictures are placed at the front of the room and each group has to argue their case for each choice of actor. Some

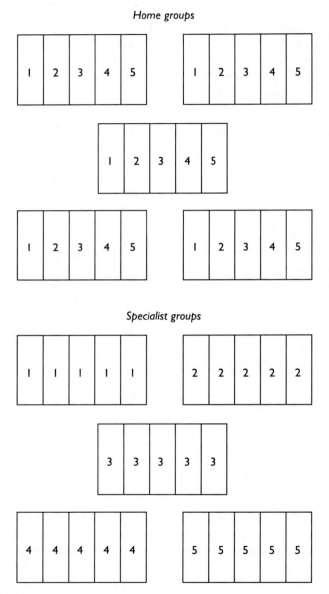

Figure 4.4 Jigsaw.

familiar faces usually stimulate extra interest. The teacher records the decisions of each group with a tally to see which actor is chosen for each role. The pupils have to use their knowledge of the play to argue their case and, if this precedes written work, it will help all students ·deepen their knowledge of character motivation and plot.

Keeping everyone on task

There is little reading involved in the activity described above and the visual stimulus makes it very accessible to different levels of ability. However, most of the pupils do have to be familiar with the play before attempting it. In challenging classrooms there will also be problems of erratic attendance to take into consideration, so revise each lesson and check groupings before moving on to the new activity. Make sure a range of pupils is speaking in the final session by careful questioning and by telling pupils that you will choose the speakers.

The key challenge is placing pupils in groups. The simplest structure for a perfect 'jigsaw' is five groups of five – 25 pupils. You can count around the room, one to five, get the pupils to write down their number and then check through each number, appointing a group leader. Another method is to give children a different coloured card to determine their group. Diagrams on the board showing the groups can help when pupils move to their groups. The resulting groups will be random and not based on friendships.

With 30 pupils you will be forced to have five groups of six, but as long as you have a mixture of characters in the final group, the children can still discuss a range of characters.

Whole class discussion/feedback

This chapter has focused on small group work but has inevitably touched on feeding back. It has been pointed out that the teacher can vary feedback by, for example, reassembling groups at the end of the lesson to share ideas from different groups and through presentations made to different audiences.

The final whole class discussion, however, can also take different forms. In a circle (or even a semi-circle), as discussed in Chapter 6, pupils will have a more equal and relaxed input in a final discussion if you can organise the seating in your classroom this way. You can also use the no-hands rule to encourage a variety of pupils to speak. The 'goldfish bowl' technique, where one group sits and discusses in the middle of a circle and the outside group comments on the discussion, is an alternative form for evaluating learning in small groups. The teacher can also discuss how well the exercise worked with the pupils.

Formal debate

Group work can also structure a whole class formal debate. A topic can be considered: for example, this class would abolish homework, and then small groups can plan the case for, the case against and each group be asked to argue their case. The topic can be placed on the board and pupils can be asked to move to the 'for' table, the 'against' table or the 'unsure' table. After group discussion, speakers can then outline their views; the class discusses and then votes. The English Speaking Union (2003) has produced some interesting resources to promote debates in schools.

Some key practical issues with small group learning in challenging classrooms

Before the lesson:

- Decide in advance how you will group the pupils, thinking carefully about ability and gender in relation to the task.
- Decide whether the groups will be working on the same or a different task
- If you need to move furniture, do it before the pupils arrive
- If you work with a teaching assistant or learning support teacher you can show them your plan and also assign them a group

During the lesson:

- Begin by revising where you are and give very clear instructions; even list the steps on the board. Brighter students will use this to remind you if you get lost!
- Use numbers and coloured cards to group the pupils when you decide not to use friendship groups
- When moving students round the room give them very clear instructions, even draw diagrams and give clear time limits for movement
- Use your regular cueing system when you want the attention of the whole group

- Avoid excessive reporting and vary the forms of feedback so that everyone is still cooperating at the end of the lesson. Make sure, however, that a summary explains what has been achieved.

After the lesson:

- Keep a record of groups by asking the pupils to write a list when you have planned for more than one oral lesson.

Keeping pupils aware of the overall aims of small group learning

The feedback from these exercises will allow for considered debate and reflection not only on the texts studied but also on the processes the pupils have gone through as they learn to share their ideas. Planning for student observers of group work can enrich feedback on how well the class worked in small groups and as a larger group. The teacher may also want to develop the discussion by asking pupils to define their own guidelines for how to work successfully in small groups, as suggested by Neil Mercer (2000). This gives them more ownership of the classroom and their rules can then be displayed in the room and referred back to when participating in these activities.

A new role for the teacher

As suggested throughout this chapter the teacher plays a facilitating and monitoring role when promoting small group work. In challenging classrooms this role will be built up slowly as you win the trust of the pupils in this new kind of lesson. The teacher must actively monitor group discussion and interaction to make sure that purposeful interaction takes place.

As students gain familiarity with these small group learning routines they will look forward to your lessons and become more knowledgeable about the texts they are studying. The ethos of excitement and endeavour, the willingness to explore and discuss through collaborative talk will engage the pupils in a different kind of learning. This approach does not treat them as empty vessels but rather values and uses their experience and knowledge to propel them forward. All pupils will make progress with these methods, and become more confident learners, from wherever they start.

Key points: Group work

- Create a climate for group work
- Link talk with direct experience
- Plan the task carefully by asking 'Is it *real* group work?' Does it have a clear outcome?
- Prepare resources and groups
- Be patient and allow for reflection
- Above all, persevere.

Chapter 5

Storytelling

> Storytelling is the direct and shared communication of something true about being alive.
>
> Simms (1982)

Oral storytelling is part of our human heritage and also a vibrant part of modern life. Not only does each life tell a story but also our daily lives are full of individual events and stories. As we meet others we relate events in our lives and tell stories about mutual friends and ourselves. The newspapers and television programmes we watch are full of stories that we discuss with each other. Sometimes we share opinions about stories we have read or programmes we have watched and in doing so begin to retell parts of the story. In the same way, pupils tell and share stories, jokes and anecdotes with each other as they move in and out of lessons, stand in the lunch queue, watch the fights and bullying in the playground and chat on the way home.

If you want to become an effective teacher in turbulent classrooms you will need to become a storyteller. The art of storytelling is often assumed to be something that teachers of younger children need. But young children are not alone in loving to listen to stories – particularly those told by people they know. You can often capture older children's interest by introducing your lesson or topic with a story. History comes alive when teachers tell stories of famous battles, kings and queens and turbulent priests. Sociology is more interesting when teachers look at case studies with pupils. Geography can focus on the human side of disasters, while science and maths become more affective subjects when the story of the famous scientist or mathematician is told. Any chapter from a book, scene from a play, verse from a poem or newspaper report can be turned into a story.

The teacher as storyteller

Every teacher can become a storyteller, but the art of storytelling involves much more than having a good memory for the storyline. The storyteller chooses the story carefully to fit the audience and engages the audience by using their voice creatively, by use of pace, silences, gestures, props and other devices which are discussed below.

The act of storytelling opens up a new relationship with your class because when we share stories, we share more of ourselves. The teacher's personality comes alive in a new form before the pupils and they start to interact with the teacher in a different way. The teacher is willing to perform, play, and the pupils automatically like it. Oral stories are a form of 'real' talk, a shared human experience. Storytelling binds people together by establishing our common humanity and also celebrates difference by drawing on a wide range of cultures and communities. You are not talking to the children to get them to do something but you are talking and telling the story for its own sake, to stimulate their imaginations and enrich their lives. A new intimacy is established in the process of storytelling. A story is more like a gift than a lesson. All the pupils have to do is listen but they are also imagining the events in the story, escaping into a new world, as they listen and they are actively constructing meaning with the teller.

The act of storytelling nearly always has a calming effect on pupils. You will feel the room relax as you begin your story and this means that disruption is less likely to occur when you choose to tell a story to the class. There are so many opportunities to tell stories in classrooms and once you start you will find that you begin to grasp new opportunities. Here are some suggestions on how to get started.

Telling jokes

The teacher tells a joke. The wide-mouth frog is popular, even if pupils have heard it before. The teacher has to put her fingers in her mouth every time she speaks as the frog and this rarely fails to amuse. The cheeky young frog goes on a journey, meeting on the way some animals in the jungle, who all have appropriate voices and are reasonably friendly until finally the frog jumps on the back of a crocodile, thinking that it is a log of wood floating in the river. The crocodile's head emerges and the little frog gets nervous.

'G-Good morning, Mr Crocodile, and what do you do every day here in the river?' asks the frog.

'Oh, I like to eat wide-mouth frogs,' replies the crocodile.

(The fingers go out of the mouth.) 'Well, you don't see many of those around nowadays,' says the frog in a very different, posh but frightened voice.

The children can then tell each other jokes and share some with the class. The teacher can set this as homework before the lesson to ensure that all can participate.

Early memories

If possible, two adults pick a theme and tell a story. An example could be a story about the day they got into trouble at school or at home. The teachers arrange the chairs in two semi-circles and sit together on a desk, in front of this semi-circle, so that they can make eye contact with all the pupils as they tell their story.

The story could, for example, include an event such as getting a slap for doing something wrong in class when at primary school. There will be many stories of corporal punishment from overseas teachers and from older teachers born in Britain. The pupils are fascinated by stories of our younger selves and enjoy hearing of how you did wrong and got into trouble. They are also particularly pleased at being told two stories on a similar theme. This is a very supportive way to start telling stories because your colleague will build on your theme and the students will appreciate your style of telling and the different voices.

This technique can lead into 'cascade' storytelling which is explained later.

Anecdotes

An anecdote about your personal experience will always engage the pupils because it differs from the normal, more formal, instructional talk of the teacher. You move into a different register and use a more informal and personal mode of address.

An example of this could be a reading lesson where you start to talk about your own attitude to books, where you read and why you like reading. One pupil asked how many books I have in my house. I started to describe each room and how many bookshelves there are in each room. The pupils piled in with more questions about the books, which were my favourites, did I throw any away, and how many books did my son have? Such an anecdote can breathe life into topics that remain dry and perhaps outside some pupils' experience. The telling of an anecdote makes a connection between your experience and the pupils' experiences.

Class surveys

If you want to give the class a stimulus for a survey of a topic such as fear, you could begin by talking about your own fears. A recurring nightmare of my youth, such as being inside the head of a skeleton and looking out through the dark holes, was a tale that one class found riveting. Another tale about a brother scaring his sister by hiding at the top of the stairs and jumping out on her, when he knew she was scared of the dark, also acted as a prompt for pupils' thoughts and experiences of fear. Their fears were shared and then a tally was listed on the board showing which were the most common fears which led to more discussion.

Traditional tales

The teacher has many choices here: myths; legends; moral tales; parables; creation stories; folk and fairy tales. The teacher needs to find stories that have strong characters, clear events and often distinguish fairly clearly between good and evil. Sometimes it will be necessary to simplify the narrative. Pupils enjoy seeing monsters and villains punished, even violently, because it allows them to feel protected from evil. The teacher will need to have key words listed or a diagram of the story as a prompt when they first tell it. You may not need to refer to this but it is a good idea to have it available, just in case.

Theseus and the Minotaur, for example, is a myth that many children are fascinated by. The idea of a 'man' who has the upper body of a bull and the lower body of a man is strange enough in itself to draw the pupils in and is often a good point to start with. The idea of a labyrinth is also mysterious and appealing. These two features can be put together and wound into the story of Theseus' triumph over the Minotaur and the consequences that follow. There are many creative activities, e.g. improvisation of particular scenes, drawing of events and characters, which can flow out of such storytelling if the teacher wishes. See Armery (1999) *Greek Myths for Young Children* for a very simple version.

Multicultural stories

The story *Underground to Canada* by Barbara Smucker tells of two young girls who dress up as boys and escape from slavery. They have to travel from Mississippi to Canada where slavery has been abolished. They are chased all the way by slave hunters and aided by abolitionists and other slaves who make up the underground railway that carries them to safety. The story, or any particular part of the story, is a rich source for storytelling. There are many historical figures, such as Harriet Tubman, whose stories can be related of real heroines who lived in the past. There are many themes that such stories raise which can form the basis for further discussion with pupils.

Classic stories

The requirement to teach from the canon of English literary heritage in the National Curriculum places enormous demands on the teacher who works in classrooms where reading ages are low and many pupils have EAL. A way of helping all students to access pre-twentieth-century literature is through storytelling.

For example, to introduce children to the setting and key characters in *The Tempest* you would start by discussing some pictures of the characters and the storm or watch the opening of the Shakespeare Animated Tales video of *The Tempest* (Stanislov, 1999). It might then be appropriate to tell younger pupils the story. Students in years 6 and 7, with lower reading ages, find it hard to concentrate on watching the video without knowing the story because the language used is quite hard to understand.

Storytelling can always be used as a device for clarifying the narrative of any Shakespeare text before pupils start to read the archaic language. Even for more able pupils this is sometimes a useful approach. There are many retellings of these stories, for example by Charles and Mary Lamb (1996), which are useful sources for the teacher who wishes to check their knowledge of these tales.

Developing storytelling techniques

There are many devices employed by professional storytellers that you may wish to integrate into your repertoire. You may find it better to adopt some of these techniques when you tell a story for a second or third time. When you are confident of the narrative you will feel most able to adapt and develop your technique.

Use of space

You need to make sure that your audience is seated in a manner and in a space that lends itself to active listening. The two semi-circles or half-moon structure outlined in the 'Early memories' section gives you eye contact with the pupils. They are sitting comfortably and you are sitting slightly above your audience.

Voice

You must speak clearly and loudly enough for your audience to hear you. Your diction must allow pupils to hear individual words clearly. You can alter the tone, pitch and volume of your voice to highlight different moods and characters in the story. You may wish to choose particularly vivid words to describe feelings, emotions or events.

Silence/pauses

You can use silence or pauses very effectively to create a sense of anticipation in your audience. You can indicate to them with your voice or body posture that this moment is integral to the telling of the story.

Movement and gesture

Movements such as walking and running, or moving towards a particular listener, can help give energy to a story. Stepping into role as different characters or lowering and then raising your head can help delineate dialogue. Using imaginary objects can lend authenticity to your tales.

Use of props

Props such as a ball of string in the Minotaur story can lend more meaning and magic to the story and thereby engage the audience more effectively. There may be a way of introducing a chair or other furniture which can help develop the imagery and setting of the story. Storytellers often carry bags or sacks with objects that they have chosen to use as part of their story.

Asking questions

At any point during the storytelling the audience can be invited to add a name to a character or event that they have previously encountered. You can also invite the audience to make up names or objects, if they can fit into your story, by asking 'What's a good name for a villain?' When you become more adept and confident or perhaps when you forget what comes next you can always ask 'And what do you think happened next?'

Refocusing the audience

Very occasionally you may have to stop your storytelling and refocus your audience. Asking questions can be one way of refocusing them. But if that is not enough you can step out of the storytelling role and explain that this is a shared experience that most pupils are enjoying and that they want to hear the rest of the story. Make it clear that this is a special event and that all pupils should show that they can appreciate it. Storytelling has such a universal appeal that this will normally be effective.

Pupils telling stories

Pupils should be encouraged to tell stories in all classrooms but in particular the most challenging ones. Oral rehearsal is vital to help pupils develop their self-confidence with language. Oral stories show pupils how stories work and how spoken language works. The process of telling a story to an audience demonstrates the power of language and adds to the status of a pupil among their peers. The teacher can bring out the links between storytelling and story writing, the use of dialogue, the description of places, the differences between colloquial and formal language, while reflecting on stories and comparing oral and written modes. Storytelling involves sharing different cultural references, allowing pupils to bring more of themselves and more of their family life into the classroom.

Cascade storytelling

This is a very simple technique for initiating pupils into storytelling. The teacher models the story and then the pupils retell the story in pairs, first as teller and then as listener. The teacher emphasises the need for pupils to face each other and be active listeners.

For example, the 'early memories' story based on autobiography can be used in this way. Two teachers tell of the day they got into trouble and then the pupils are told to think of a time when they got into trouble. They are then asked to turn to their partner and tell their story to each other on this theme. The teachers might like to use another early memory such as having an accident; the pupils then repeat the exercise with a different title. After this the teacher asks for volunteers to come to the front to tell the story of their choice. There is never any shortage of volunteers; you will have to return to this in the next lesson, as the pupils are very eager to tell their rehearsed stories.

This exercise can lead to writing if the teacher feels it is appropriate. Some of the most powerful writing by pupils in London, from schools in areas of social disadvantage, has been autobiographical.

Key-moment storytelling

This builds on the previous example, only this time a key moment is chosen first by the teacher and then by the pupils. Some pupils will choose the same moment but others will choose their own. To make this more descriptive you can ask pupils to visualise the moment or turn on the TV sets inside their heads and tell their partner exactly what they see.

One-minute storytelling

This is a delightful way of making storytelling even more fun and more of a challenge by eventually reducing the time in which to tell the story to just one minute. Boys have responded particularly well to this exercise.

For example, you give out a ten-point summary of the story of *Macbeth* before the pupils have read the play. They are told they have four minutes to read and summarise the plot. They are then told to turn to their partner and retell the story in five minutes. You then ask their partner to tell the story in four minutes. You then ask them to repeat the exercise with one of them telling the story in two minutes. The teacher stops the activity and asks if there is anyone in the room who can manage to tell the whole story in one minute. There is usually one volunteer and they often manage to do it to great acclaim. This exercise was also thoroughly enjoyed by staff in a training session outlined in Chapter 11.

Cartoon storytelling

This uses pupils' visual memory to draw a cartoon picture or storyboard of the story they have just heard. The pupils are asked to listen carefully and then draw, for example, a six-frame cartoon. They then use this as the basis for telling their story to the class. The choices pupils make about their frames will show that each individual interprets a story differently and finds their own meaning in the story.

Ping-pong storytelling

This involves two pupils telling a story by batting words from one to another. One pupil starts with 'The' and the next pupil adds 'boy'. The first pupil then adds 'put' and so it continues until one person cannot think of a word. A whole class can do this in a circle and the activity can be changed from words to sentences.

Make up your own ending

The teacher tells a story and reaches the climax and then asks the pupils in pairs to consider how the story might end. Pupils are then grouped into fours to compare their different endings and reflect on why they may have come to different or similar endings. The whole class can then discuss which ending they prefer and the teacher can tell the class the 'real' ending or the choice the original teller made.

Tableaux storytelling

This exercise involves a group of children constructing a series of freeze-frames for the story or one frame for a key moment in the story. One pupil will have to sculpt the other pupils into a tableau or picture of the moment and position them and tell them what gestures to make. This has links with cartoon storytelling and allows the pupils to move about to frame their picture. The exercise naturally lends itself to other drama activities such as role play, interior monologue, which is outlined in Chapter 7, and it can lead into creative writing or making scripts if the teacher wishes to take the storytelling in that direction.

Scaffolding for learners new to English

Many of these storytelling activities have been attempted with EAL pupils, but there are ways to scaffold them for pupils who are *very* new to English. The teacher models the talk in all cases which gives pupils a framework for their story. The pupils can tell their stories in their heritage language. Picture prompts can always support a retelling of a story and help pupils to sequence a story with which they may be less familiar. Dual-language books, videos and tapes of stories can be taken home or listened to prior to, parallel to or as a follow up to these exercises, as storytelling encourages reading for pleasure. EAL pupils will also enjoy just listening to their peers tell stories as it introduces them to many different cultural reference points. A second adult can always retell the story in the lesson so that pupils hear it twice. They might be given pictures or objects to support their storytelling. Stories have universal features across cultures and EAL pupils will often be familiar with a story in a different form and become willing to tell their own stories.

This chapter does not include a specific section on keeping everyone on task because, of all the small group talk activities described in this book, storytelling is the most natural form of talk. Storytelling is prompted or scaffolded by the teacher but it does not have to be taught from scratch. Disruptive behaviour is less likely to occur in such lessons. Storytelling helps us all to express our identity and allows for emotional engagement; it also releases and extends our imagination.

Bruner (1996) argues that it is 'only in the narrative mode that one can construct an identity and find a place in one's culture'. While story-telling develops language skills, it also enhances pupils' social and emotional development. When pupils experience this mode of teaching and are allowed this form of personal expression, the shared experience will act to strengthen the bonds between pupils and increase trust.

Key points: Storytelling

- Storytelling is a very natural form of communication; it is 'real talk'
- Storytelling allows pupils to relax and engage at a more emotional, expressive level
- Storytelling develops pupils' knowledge about language and about stories/literature
- Storytelling aids EAL pupils and can celebrate different cultural experiences
- Teachers should experiment with stories they are very familiar with and build up their storytelling techniques
- Teachers can use stories as a stimulus for talk, for drama and for creative writing.

Chapter 6

Drama for the non-specialist

> Bruner suggests that a learner needs to participate actively in the learning process and that a child's feelings, fantasies and values need to be incorporated into lessons so that knowledge becomes personalised.
>
> Bowell and Heap (2001)

Drama lessons are often greatly admired when taught by drama specialists, but other teachers, even English teachers, have a great fear of drama. This is understandable if you have not been trained to teach this subject and these fears are exacerbated in challenging classrooms because of the problems of behaviour management. It is hard enough to keep the pupils on task with the formal layout of chairs and desks but in a drama lesson these formal 'props' are absent. If you actually dare to take children into the drama room there will be no possibility of regaining control through writing at desks.

English teachers are often asked to teach drama when there is no specialist available. The fears about drama teaching run parallel to many of the anxieties about group work but in many instances they are stronger. The core principles of drama include cooperation and communication while the core unit is often the group which means that drama activities require similar skills to those being used in group work. But drama also requires teachers to manage the whole group in a wide range of new and unfamiliar contexts. It is only by teachers experiencing the success of drama activities and the positive impact they can have on students that these fears will be overcome.

The case for taking a great leap forward with drama in challenging contexts is, however, very compelling:

- Drama is a popular subject among many pupils. Both boys and girls respond well to drama lessons with clear structures and clear outcomes. Many boys are particularly enthusiastic about well-structured drama lessons.
- Drama conventions give pupils a secure framework in which to experiment and play with communication.
- Drama allows students to move about. This is of great benefit to lively pupils who can learn how to focus their energy and improve their physical coordination.
- Drama can act as therapy, allowing pupils to confront feelings and problems they may have suppressed.
- Drama can give expression to our feelings and emotions and develops the artistic and aesthetic impulses in us all.
- Drama encourages personal responses, allows for different interpretations and develops a critical approach to literature.
- Drama encourages pupils to make considered judgements and helps prepare them for adult life.
- Drama, through acting and writing in role, can extend the range and develop the quality of pupils' speech and writing.
- Drama enhances cooperation and self-discipline and allows pupils to give and receive constructive criticism.
- Drama provides opportunities for both highly literate and less literate pupils to excel.

The tasks outlined below have been selected because they have all been used successfully with challenging groups of students. The activities have taken place in classrooms, the drama studio, the school hall or the school library. The tasks are divided into two categories so that teachers can start with shorter, more gentle drama activities and then move on to more sustained activities and even whole class drama lessons.

It is recommended that you build up your drama-teaching repertoire slowly. It is assumed that the reader has not been trained as a drama teacher and therefore this chapter starts with reading activities and role play and moves on to forms of drama that use a wider range of conventions and are more sustained. The pupils will gain confidence alongside you. In a secondary school and in some junior schools you may have drama timetabled as a separate subject, so making links with the drama teacher will be of great benefit for discussion, gaining a wider knowledge of drama conventions and, best of all, for team teaching. You can also ask your department or head teacher to invite drama groups into school to perform or run workshops with pupils.

Stage one: gentle drama

Group play reading

This is probably a good place for teachers new to drama to start. It involves a group of students working together to perform part of a play.

- Choose a scene from a play; pupils or teachers can choose.
- Tell the pupils to make a list of the characters in the scene. The teacher may wish to appoint a pupil or get the groups to choose one pupil to chair the discussion.
- Remind the students that acting involves thinking about use of space, where the actors will stand, how they will speak and use gestures. The teacher may wish to model this with a couple of pupils and yourself in role for a couple of lines.
- Tell the pupils to decide which members of their group are going to play the parts.
- Get each group to talk about the characters and what they do in the scene they have chosen.
- Tell the pupils to read and rehearse the scene. Make sure that all groups get out of their seats so they can act and move about.
- Ask a couple of groups to act out the scene for the rest of the class.

Example

The teacher is half-way through reading *Gregory's Girl* by Bill Forsyth, a play about dating and adolescence. The teacher asks the groups to choose their favourite scene so far and then suggests they pick the most dramatic moment to act out. There may be common favourites, such as the scene where the boys watch the nurses change clothes, but different groups will approach scenes differently.

Keeping everyone on task

There will immediately be a debate about who reads which part. You will need to make it clear that they have a time limit to decide who plays which part. The role of chair or director may need clarifying. With very low-age readers you will need to find simple play scripts for them to read. As suggested in the idea of Guided Reading, outlined in the National Literacy and Key Stage 3 strategies (1998, 2003), you may wish to work directly with one of these groups to help EAL pupils to decode and understand new words. If you can anticipate these needs by having key words written on the board at the beginning of the lesson, this will also help low-age readers. You may decide to have only one or two groups performing before the whole class but all the pupils will have experienced dramatic reading and learnt more about the play and how to communicate effectively.

Simple dramatic readings

- The teacher reads a poem or passage, projecting her voice with some emphasis and change of tone and pace where appropriate.
- The pupils are asked to identify and discuss the reading techniques the teacher has used and why she used them.
- The pupils are told to re-read the poem. They are placed in groups and told to prepare a dramatic reading in their groups.
- Two or three groups perform their dramatic reading and give reasons for their choice of techniques.
- The teacher encourages pupils to reflect on why the readings were effective and make comparisons between different approaches.

Example

The teacher could read a poem such as *The Lesson* by Roger McGough which starts 'Chaos ruled in the classroom as gaily the teacher walked in'. This is a humorous poem about a teacher trying to deal with a chaotic and violent class. The teacher will need to think about how they read the poem aloud. They might begin to shout when they come to the point where the teacher in the poem is shouting at their class and change their voice and persona to express fear when speaking as a pupil threatened by the teacher later on in the poem. The teacher may use gesture when they have a sword in their hand in another verse. The pace of the reading may change at particular points.

Keeping everyone on task

You can choose a poem that is slightly above the reading level of some of the pupils in the class if the poet's message is appropriate for the audience. When this technique is first introduced, the groupings should include a range of reading abilities. The teacher will need to organise this spread of ability and circulate to help some groups clarify key words or lines where necessary. Mixed ability groupings are rarely completely evenly matched. Once again the teacher may decide to work with one particular group, once the class is fully engaged, in making their choice and preparing the reading.

At a later stage, when the pupils have become familiar with this approach, the teacher could extend the activity by giving each group of pupils a number of poems on a theme to choose from.

Another approach to dramatic reading and developing pupils' skills of oral interpretation is *Learning with Reader's Theatre* (Dixon, *et al.* 1996). This involves taking any text and turning it into a play by marking the text in different colours for different voices. It creates roles such as narrator, characters 1, 2 and 3, that the readers can identify in the margin, and gives the group a script to perform.

Key word dramatic reading

In this technique pupils are introduced to a poem by choosing a key word that they are asked to read aloud in different voices.

- The teacher places or types a large copy of the poem on the whiteboard
- The teacher asks the pupils to choose any word in the poem
- The teacher underlines the words that the pupils have chosen
- The teacher then gets pupils to call out their words as she points to them
- The teacher does this slowly, quickly, asks the pupils to speak softly, loudly, in a happy or sad voice or uses a pattern or rhythm with the words
- The pupils enjoy this activity and the teacher can question them about their choice of words. Why did they choose their word? Which tone of voice was most appropriate for their word? This naturally leads into a discussion about the poet's choices, the imagery and mood of the poem and what they think the poet's message might be
- The teacher then reads the poem.

Example

A poem such as *First Ice* by the Russian poet Andre Voznesensky (1985), about a girl freezing in a telephone booth while being stood up by her boyfriend, will allow pupils to choose words such as ice or icy which emphasise the cold, sad mood of the poem. The girl has been rejected for the first time and it hurts. The children will make choices based on the repetition of words such as ice and icy and the way these words echo the sad mood of the poem and the girl's feelings at that moment. They will also make choices based on the sound and visual impact of words such as glitter, with reference to the frozen tears on her cheeks. Another feature of their choices will be finding the pattern of sounds such as the alliteration at the beginning of the words freezing, face, fingers, first.

Keeping everyone on task

You need a long stick to point at words and make sure your instructions are very specific when asking the pupils to say their words. Reading one word of their choice makes this an accessible task for most students. If students choose the same word they can read together.

Role-on-the-wall

This is a highly visual device for allowing pupils to reflect more deeply on a character by drawing a large outline of the character's head and shoulders and writing statements around the drawing:

- Draw an outline of a character's head and shoulders on a large piece of paper
- Show the pupils how to choose statements that the character has made and copy them around the outline of the character
- Then ask the pupils to tell the teacher what that character is really thinking and write words that describe the inner feelings inside the head of the character in the drawing. Explain that the pupils can use the first person as they write about the character's feelings
- The pupils are then asked to choose a different character and design a role-on-the-wall diagram for this character.

This activity can produce excellent displays for the classroom and furnish material for future hot-seating activities.

Example

Figure 6.1 shows a role-on-the-wall diagram for the story *Lamb to the Slaughter* by Roald Dahl. Patrick Maloney, the detective, is just about to tell his pregnant wife that he is leaving her. This is a tense, dramatic moment in this otherwise amusing short story. The role-on-the-wall

Lamb to the Slaughter by Roald Dahl

This records the moment before the revenge of Mrs Maloney when Mr Maloney tells his wife he will have to leave her.

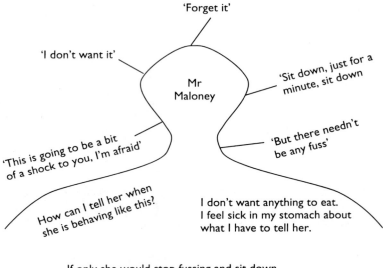

Figure 6.1 Role-on-the-wall.

activity could be a self-contained exercise to clarify understanding of the story at that moment. It could also be used to prepare some creative playwriting where pupils imagine exactly what Patrick said to Mary at this point in the story and write out their own script.

Keeping everyone on task

Make sure you have plenty of felt-tip pens to allow pupils to use different colours for inner and outer thoughts. Ensure you count out the pens and count them in again. If you find that some groups are still having problems finding quotations, ask those who are managing to explain to others to give examples of what they have found and how they found the statements. Pupils explaining how they have tackled the task is a very effective way of ensuring that everyone completes the task successfully.

Character hot-seating

This is a device that puts a character in a chair to be questioned by others in the group. The pupil in the 'hot seat' has to answer in the first person as if they were that character. The exercise builds on the previous exercise of role-on-the-wall as it allows pupils to gain a deeper understanding of a character's motivation. The pupils will be more confident in role if it is planned in stages. For example:

- The teacher can start by modelling hot-seating by becoming a character in a story with which the class is familiar and asking pupils or other adults to ask her questions. Their teacher becoming someone else will immediately entertain the pupils. They realise that their teacher is willing to play with roles and language and take risks. As a result the teacher often gains more control of the group by moving into role.
- She then explains that all the pupils will be working in role as a character and that some pupils will be questioned at the end of the lesson. This is a similar exercise to the interviews in role previously explained in Chapter 3 on Paired Talk.
- The teacher can give some examples of questions that may be asked (see Figure 6.2) or help the pupils to make up questions.
- The teacher then reads a passage and asks the pupils to think about a particular character.
- The teacher may then choose to brainstorm this character's traits or concerns or use a role-on-the-wall poster to talk about the character.
- The pupils work as partners to question each other in role.
- The teacher then asks for volunteers to hot-seat in turn and be questioned.
- The teacher can start the questioning and allow the class to take over or let the class ask all the questions if they are confident in this technique.

Keeping everyone on task

If this activity starts in pairs it becomes accessible to most pupils. There may be pupils new to English who need the prompt of an adult or picture prompts to help them get into role. The teacher needs to be

---

Character hot-seating

---

1 Discuss what has been happening to your character and how they are likely to be feeling at this point in the play.

---

2 Now ask each other the following questions. Answer in role.

- Could you describe how you feel at this point?

- Did you feel at the centre of what has just gone on or on the edges?

- Were you generally leading and directing the dialogue and action or were you mainly reacting to it?

- Were there things you wanted to do during that scene that you didn't?

- Were there things you wanted to say but didn't?

- What is making you behave as you are right now?

- What is important to you at the moment?

- Make a note of any questions you would like to ask the other characters at this point.

Figure 6.2 Questions to characters in role.

flexible about this and respond as necessary. If the teacher feels it is necessary, two pupils can be asked to demonstrate the opening of their conversation to reinforce the task. The teacher may want to put pairs into fours for the reporting back stage to allow for more participation. Then one group of four might volunteer to show their work.

This activity can be extended by asking pupils to choose from a range of characters. The feedback can then involve a panel of different characters. Another way of extending the activity is for the teacher, during the questioning of the character, to move into role as, for example, a film director and ask pupils questions about how they might perform that role on screen. This allows the teacher to adopt the *mantle of the expert* – another drama convention with which the pupils will become familiar – and allows you to create other 'expert' roles such as historian, social worker, TV producer for them in other lessons.

Use of props

Using objects to demonstrate a concept or idea or to highlight an event in a story or poem is another very effective way of gaining the pupils' attention and deepening their understanding. Masks, hats, scarves, etc.

can be useful for adopting different roles. Other objects can be used just to illustrate a particular point. The use of props gives pupils visual cues to aid their understanding of concepts and narratives. The pupils are always entertained by their teacher and fellow students performing even a short piece of drama.

Example

Untitled Poem by Simon Armitage (1998), about burning a girl's hands in a science lesson, has much more impact if acted out beforehand with an imaginary flame coming from a real Bunsen burner and a pair of scissors whose handles are placed in the flame and then passed to a student in role as the girl in the poem. The girl can react as if she really has been burnt and the teacher can use the drama to discuss what happened and why it might have happened before the actual reading of the poem.

Keeping everyone on task

The familiarity of the objects used makes this an accessible activity. Health and safety warnings may be necessary with the use of Bunsen burners. Drawing and the use of props are often very accessible cues to stimulate interest in and understanding of poems and other texts.

Stage two: more sustained drama activities

Simulations with roles

These are life events or situations that are reproduced to allow students to engage in a decision-making process. The groups are usually set a deadline for making their decision. Roles for characters written on cards, which have a picture and/or description of the character, can be used to clarify the exercise.

Example

A 'cash and choice' simulation can allow students to work in different roles to consider how resources are spent in a school. The groups are given a total amount they can spend and then asked to make a choice about what they should spend it on: for example, a refurbished gym, computer suite, redecoration of the building, etc. Each item is costed so that the pupils have to make choices within the budget. The pupils can be asked to work as the school council, a parent group, a staff working party or a group of governors and compare their choices at the end. For further ideas on this exercise see the English and Media Centre booklet on *School* (Stephens and Simmons, 1990).

Keeping everyone on task

The roles need to be clarified and a brainstorm or character role cards will allow pupils to move into their designated roles successfully. The teacher could break the groups up after the discussion and get them to work with another group on making comparisons about their different choices. The teacher could then lead a productive whole class discussion about why these different choices have been made. The structure for the reporting back should engage the class as it involves a new level of thinking about the choices made. As with all group tasks, the teacher will need to support groups who are slow to get started or need clarification.

Freeze-frame

When we discussed the use of the moving image to engage pupils at the beginning of a lesson, freeze-frame meant pressing the pause button on the screen. But in drama freeze-frame involves pupils sculpting that moment as if they were statues of the characters in the play, story, poem, conversation, advert or picture. One person can act as the sculptor to create the frozen image and place individuals in the right pose and position. A passage or picture from a text can be used or a freeze-frame of a video or DVD as a stimulus. The teacher might ask the pupils to sculpt two contrasting moments in the story.

Example

A dramatic moment in a play, such as the scene in *A View from the Bridge* where Marco challenges his belligerent cousin, Eddie, to lift a chair from its base with one hand, can be acted out. This action acts as a warning to Eddie, as it is an attempt to stop him trying to ridicule and intimidate his younger brother.

- The pupils read and act out this moment.
- The teacher then works with one group and helps them to sculpt the scene.

- The teacher demonstrates and then asks each group to copy this with one member of the group acting as the sculptor.
- A discussion can then take place of the different choices the sculptors have made. The teacher might even ask some of the pupils to follow this up by writing their thoughts down in role.

Keeping everyone on task

The teacher can arrange this activity as an introduction to the play or as a performance activity after reading the first act. The pupils should have one chance to read this excerpt from the play before they perform. They need to have some understanding of the significance of the moment. The teacher may wish to teach the idea of dramatic tension as part of the preparation for this activity. The groups benefit from having a range of reading abilities so that any difficulties can be overcome through peer collaboration. Chairs can be available or imagined.

Interior monologue

It is very natural to extend the freeze-frame activity by introducing interior monologue to consider what might be going through the character's mind at that moment. Each character might come alive and speak their thoughts or another pupil may speak the inner thoughts for that character.

Example

A group that has sculpted the freeze-frame from the scene above is asked to think about and then speak the thoughts that might be going through each character's head at that moment. You can always prompt them or demonstrate one character's thoughts yourself. The teacher should then ask the other groups to copy this technique and a couple of performances could ensue. This piece of drama could lead into an extended monologue for a character at several moments of the play. It can produce extended, high-quality writing in role; for example, a piece of original writing entitled 'Eddie's Monologue'.

Keeping everyone on task

The modelling of the activities by the teacher and the students can provide a firm framework for all pupils to succeed in drama activities. If the pupils know exactly what you want them to do, they will succeed. The teacher needs to look for the groups that need extra support and scaffolding. The teacher also needs to ask a few probing questions at the evaluation stage which get the pupils to articulate the reasons behind the different choices they have made.

A new dimension can be added at the evaluation stage by considering *the playwright's viewpoint*, by asking where the playwright might be standing. Nearer to Eddie or Marco?

Guided tour

This is an activity that involves blindfolding one pupil and asking another pupil to guide them around an imaginary space in the classroom. The teacher could start with a brainstorm of the particular place they will be visiting.

Example

After watching the storm in the video of *The Tempest*, you could ask pupils to imagine that they are on the boat. The teacher could brainstorm the different parts of the ship, using nautical terms where appropriate. A picture from the text would assist the brainstorm. A pupil could then begin to guide the teacher around the ship when it is sailing in calm waters. The teacher would start to ask questions such as: 'Can you tell me what I am walking towards?' 'What colour is it?' 'What shape is it?' The teacher then asks a pupil to take her place and the tour continues.

Keeping everyone on task

The video and picture would assist the pupils in imagining a sailing vessel at that time. This would help stimulate the language needed for this particular exercise. The teacher might also decide to read the opening pages of the Shakespeare Animated Tales version of *The Tempest* to help set the scene. The fun of guiding the teacher should initially engage the class. You can play safe and just close your eyes if you prefer not to be blindfolded.

Choric reading

This activity involves using drama conventions, such as movement, mime and space to create a context or a mood, to read just a few lines of

Elizabethan language. Students are encouraged to read individual lines aloud together, chorically like a choir, to scaffold the use of Shakespeare's language. This technique builds on the choric reading that takes place in the early years of primary school where children read a big book together during shared reading sessions. Choric or shared reading is very supportive to EAL pupils and pupils with low reading ages.

Example

In introducing Shakespeare's *The Tempest*, the teacher can use the five senses (touch, taste, sound, smell, sight) to bring the ship alive in the storm through the use of movement, mime, a sound track and eventually the choric reading of lines from the text.

- The class watches the storm scene at the beginning of the Shakespeare Animated Tales video of *The Tempest*, or another film version, or looks closely at the pictures in the text.
- The class brainstorms each of the five senses.
- The teacher asks what can we hear on the ship as the storm rises? What can we see, smell, touch and taste? This can be done in groups or as a whole class.
- The teacher then puts pupils into groups of four or five. The pupils are told that the group must become the boat by sculpting themselves into a still image of it.
- They then have to start moving and, as the storm rises, they make the sounds of the storm. The sounds get louder as the storm rages and then dies down. The groups practise being the boat in the storm.
- The teacher then passes round a few lines cut out from the play which the pupils have to read and then add at the appropriate moment.
- One or two groups are then invited to perform their reading of the storm.

The dramatic devices used help the pupils to read a small amount of archaic language. The lines can come from the original play or *Shakespeare: The Animated Tales*, retold by Leon Garfield (1992). This activity can be used as a stimulus for descriptive writing, artwork and poetry based on the storm and to stimulate discussion on the magic at work in creating the storm. For more ideas on choric reading of Shakespeare's plays, see Peter Reynolds's *Practical Approaches to Shakespeare* (1991).

Keeping everyone on task

Two adults are useful in this exercise as they can circulate and help the groups sculpt their boat and practise the movement. With clear modelling and guidance, however, one teacher can work with a whole class. The teacher must focus on the process of creating the boat and help pupils to sculpt their image and their movements carefully. Starting with a practice in slow motion or freeze-frame and then moving the pace on can work well.

Conscience corridor/advice circle

This involves pupils giving advice to a character about a decision they are about to make. The pupils can form two lines and offer contrasting advice to a character or sit round the character in a circle and offer more thoughtful advice.

Example

Reading a later chapter of *Great Expectations*, when Magwitch arrives at the older Pip's lodgings, you can read a little of Pip's first reactions of disdain. A film version can also underline this reaction. Discuss the justice of Pip's reactions with the class and then set up a series of advice circles where one pupil becomes Pip and the other pupils offer Pip advice on how he should react to Magwitch.

Keeping everyone on task

Make sure the pupils are absolutely clear about what they have to do. Give the pupils the opportunity to reflect on what they already know about the characters' relationship in the class discussion or through questioning as you read the passage. Get one group to demonstrate with you as a member of the advice circle what you want each group to do. This scaffolds the exercise for the pupils new to English and gives them a clear idea of how to phrase their advice. This exercise was derived from materials in Webster's *Studying Great Expectations* (2004).

Forum theatre

This activity also involves the pupils giving advice but this time the advice is given while a small group acts out a scenario and the group watches. The group watching can stop the action whenever they feel it is losing direction or if they need help. Observers can step in and act in role to illustrate their advice.

Example

A group of children ask to meet the head teacher to discuss improving school dinners. The head explains that there is a limited amount of cash available and that they will have to make out a strong case for spending the money on this rather than other resources. The observers help construct the argument with the group working as actors.

Keeping everyone on task

This kind of activity would need to take place with a group that has some exposure to drama-based lessons, as the audience will be larger than the group involved in the drama. The pupils will need to have the rules of the activity explained and their role as an active audience made clear before the activity takes place.

Teacher-in-role in whole class drama

The teacher steps into role as a character in a given scenario over several lessons in order to direct the drama and deepen the pupils' thinking. All the pupils have to be involved. Where the role is a directive one, as with the judge in the example below, you will again be surprised by how much your authority increases. This is because the exercise creates a structure in which all participants can perform a different role.

Example

- The teacher can become a judge in the trial of, for example, Marco after he has killed Eddie at the end of *A View from the Bridge* by Arthur Miller. The teacher prepares the scenario by asking some pupils to refer back to the play and in pairs to outline the case for Marco's defence. She asks others to prepare the case for the prosecution.
- The teacher asks for pupils to volunteer for roles as officers of the court, lawyers and witnesses. She asks them to think about what they will say in court.
- When the trial begins, the teacher walks into the room with a large

mallet to act as a gavel. (The trial takes place in America and therefore gavels are allowed.)

- As soon as she enters the room the court is asked to rise and the teacher has become a judge.
- She introduces herself formally and reads out the charges. This sets the scene and the court drama begins.

Keeping everyone on task

The problems with this activity are sometimes unusual ones. The pupils want the trial to go on forever and you have to limit the number of witnesses. You also need to allow the jury to have an open discussion at the end to make the jury's role more interesting. In some cases there will be strong competition for the parts of the lawyers and you may need to rotate these parts. In mixed classrooms, you also need to think about the gender of the lawyers, as boys are the most likely to volunteer quickly. If you can get an MRO or colleague to video part of the trial, the recording can be used for an evaluation of the activity.

Some more generic issues in drama lessons

A drama lesson?

By this stage you are almost at the level of a full drama lesson. Several of these later activities could become full drama lessons by being structured in the following way.

The stages of a drama lesson might be:

- Games/warm up
- Engagement/establishing a scenario/modelling
- Group activity
- Performance
- Evaluation.

Examples of drama games

There are many teaching guides which give advice on drama games or warm ups to get pupils ready for the different atmosphere of a drama lesson. A few examples are listed below.

Keeper of the keys

A pupil sits on a chair with a scarf covering their eyes. The teacher quietly places a set of keys under the chair and points to a member of the group sitting in the large circle around the pupil. The pupil from the circle has to try and get the keys without the keeper of the keys hearing their movement.

Body-based Chinese whispers

The pupils stand in a line. The teacher holds her arm out and then lets it relax. The students have to copy her. The last pupil shows the action to see if it has changed. She goes to the end of the line. The next study produces a body motion which the pupils have to copy. This carries on until a number of students have led the group.

The name game

The pupils stand in a large circle. The teacher points to a pupil, says her own name and changes places. She then tells the pupils to take over and steps out of the circle. The pupil who says the name of the person they are looking at rather than their own name is out. The game continues until only a few participants are left.

Games of this type encourage pupils to value movement, body language, eye contact and close listening as forms of communication. They also improve group cooperation.

Getting the pupils into groups

Given that the group is the core of the drama lesson, teachers have devised interesting ways of getting pupils into groups that make it a game and allow movement. For example, get the pupils to walk around the room slowly, then clap your hands and tell them to find a partner. Next ask the pupils to hop around the room and then get into threes. Finally, ask them to walk in slow motion and then start running and then quickly clap and ask them to find a five. This way you can establish groups with different combinations and get pupils to work with each other.

Cueing

The advice given in Chapter 2 on using a clear cueing system to gain the pupils' attention is obviously particularly important in a drama lesson. The drama teacher often uses the hands-up signal to get everyone to stop and listen. The teacher may wish to practise this drill or their chosen cueing system at the beginning of drama sessions, as it is vital that you are able to draw the pupils back to you when you need them to listen. When the teacher is in role and the pupils are off task, the teacher has to step out of role as a cue to refocus the group.

How to begin and end

Drama lessons and workshops often begin and end in a circle. This formation allows everyone to have eye contact and places the teacher in a more equal role in relation to the students. For beginning the lesson, for reflection during or at the end of the lesson the circle is often used as it can create a calm, supportive and reflective moment for the pupils to share thoughts and ideas. In drama questioning allows for pupils to use higher-order skills and Figure 6.3 suggests some questions that might be used during the evaluation of drama activities.

This chapter has attempted to give the non-specialist drama teacher some practical advice on how to introduce, first, smaller and then more sustained drama activities into lessons. The teacher who attempts to use some of these activities will find that pupils become more adept at using their own experience of the world as a resource for their learning. The scaffolding provided by drama conventions allows pupils to take risks, create their own rules and discover their own voices. NATE has produced some excellent resources, such as the NATE drama pack (2005), for promoting drama in schools.

The references for the literature referred to in this chapter are listed at the end of this book, but it is hoped that the activities and drama conventions described here will be used with texts of the teacher's choice, ones that they have enjoyed reading. If a teacher does attempt some of these activities, the relationship with the class will change. The texts the pupils study can be lifted off the page and made more accessible. Most of the pupils will start to anticipate these lessons and you will be eagerly asked in the corridor, 'Are we are going to the hall today, Miss?'

Questions are used in drama before, during and after a piece of work is shown to stimulate discussion of each other's work, generate a supportive and inclusive working environment, and to develop practical ideas and skills to a higher level.

Open:
What did you do this weekend?
What skills did they use in their drama?

Closed:
Did you have a good weekend?
Did you like the still image?

If a group is particularly uncommunicative or unsupportive of each other, follow the 'One good thing...' rule.

The following questions could be asked following a role-play where a teenage boy has been caught by his father trying to sneak into the house well after his curfew.

Types of questions

1. Analysis
How old was your character?
Were you in the living room or kitchen?
How could he have shown that? (to audience)
What time was it? What makes you say that?

2. Form
What did the way he moved tell you about how he felt about being late?
How was the father sitting when the child came in late?
How do we know he is not telling the truth?

3. Inference
Where do you think he'd been?
Do you think he was supposed to have been out that late?
Was he drunk?

4. Evaluation
How effective was the use of space/levels/body language/facial expression?
What would the effect have been if the characters had been further apart?
How might the scene have been different if the character had been a girl?

5. Analogous
It's like when your dad's late home from work and his tea has been burnt. Can you think of any other situation when you haven't wanted to get caught?

6. Hypotheses
What if he had come in with his arm in a sling?

7. Synthesis (two ideas together to generate a third)
What if he had come in with his arm in a sling, but winked to the audience?

Figure 6.3 Drama questions for evaluation.

Key points: Drama for the non-specialist

- Drama is one of the most popular subjects in schools
- Both the least and the most literate can excel at drama
- Pupils enjoy experimenting with language and feelings in a safe environment
- Teachers should start with some gentle drama activities based on texts and build up their drama-teaching repertoire
- Drama promotes reader response and critical thinking
- Drama lessons reinforce group identity and group cooperation.

Chapter 7

Special Educational Needs and talk

> Schools assume and reflect a middle class culture with literacy at its heart, whilst kids from working class families are part of a culture that has not literacy at its heart, but oracy.
>
> Willy Russell (1991)

In junior and secondary schools where social disadvantage is widespread there is quite a large group of working-class children who are defined as having Special Educational Needs (SEN) due to low levels of literacy and poor concentration skills or poor cognitive skills. These pupils are grouped in the School Action Plus category on the SEN register. As such these pupils receive support from outside of the school, e.g. an educational psychologist has made assessments of the pupils.

'Comprehensive' schools, with only a small number of pupils from disadvantaged backgrounds, have far fewer children in this particular category, although they may have quite a few pupils with full statements. Sometimes schools are more willing to incorporate intelligent pupils with physical difficulties, who have full statements, over pupils who fit into the more potentially 'disruptive' Action Plus category. In order to address the needs of these pupils it is important that teachers understand the educational context within which they are working otherwise they will just see these pupils as 'difficult'.

Differences between schools in different areas have existed ever since comprehensive schools were established but, with the promotion of parental choice by successive governments and concessions that allow more schools to select pupils, the social segregation of schools is increasing. Educational charities have highlighted this process of social selection by comparing, in one area, the small number of pupils receiving free school meals in Church schools with the much higher number in some

Community schools. In large cities the schools with high numbers of pupils receiving free school meals are sometimes defined as 'sink' schools. Often these schools are undersubscribed and are therefore the schools where you will find a large number of pupils on this part of the SEN register. Pupils who are suspended from other schools sometimes find a place in these schools. The alienation of these pupils often increases as they travel through the school system and they become more aware of their poor literacy skills and how this is hampering their success.

The School Action Plus pupil does not have a full statement, as do some pupils with very severe learning, behavioural or physical needs. The school will, however, receive extra funds for this group of children and some hours of reading support may be available for a group or individuals to work with a teaching assistant or learning mentor. However, the primary responsibility for educating these pupils rests with the class teacher. Funding arrangements for Special Educational Needs are changing and some money is allocated to schools with high numbers of pupils receiving free school meals and with larger numbers of pupils in the School Action Plus category.

However, teachers do not receive extra payment for working with these pupils as they used to when a Social Priority Allowance was attached to a teacher's salary. There is no longer the kind of funding available to these schools in, for example, London that there was when the Inner London Education Authority (ILEA) was responsible for school financing. The ILEA financing system encouraged richer boroughs to subsidise education in poorer boroughs. In general today, these schools, where social disadvantage predominates, have less money than Beacon schools, Foundation schools and City Academies. While in the past a Special Needs teacher, with a special allowance, often supported these pupils, a less well-paid teaching assistant now supports them. Even the schools that serve these children are pressured, by the ever-present threat of league table results, to devote more resources to their higher ability pupils, who may achieve a C grade or above at GCSE. Consequently, it is sometimes the case that less resources are allocated to these pupils.

This chapter will discuss a specific case study of such a group of pupils, showing how they responded to a particular lesson based on talk called the 'Alien Coat Game' and contrast their response with that of a higher set.

Much of this book has dealt implicitly with the needs of these pupils and EAL pupils. Earlier chapters have emphasised that such pupils will need to be trained to listen and talk for smaller talk tasks before the teacher engages in more adventurous approaches. This chapter tries to address the needs of SEN pupils more explicitly and describe their responses in a more ambitious lesson. By using this case study approach it is hoped that teachers will be encouraged to consider talk-based lessons for similar groups of pupils when they feel the pupils are ready for such activities.

This Year 7 class was the fourth set in a five-set year group in an all-boys secondary school in a very poor area of London. A high proportion of pupils were on free school meals and attendance was below average. The reading ages of the group were 7–8½ years old. The majority of pupils were Afro-Caribbean; one pupil was a new arrival from Jamaica. There were two pupils with EAL, one from Turkey and one from Sri Lanka.

Two of the three white pupils in the class placed immense demands on the teacher. One pupil had extreme difficulties with handwriting and the other displayed highly challenging behaviour. The latter pupil would arrive in the room and almost immediately try and start a fight or often just run around the room. On one occasion this child started to try and climb up the wall. This pupil had recently experienced an unpleasant parental break-up and his father had tried to kidnap him a couple of times. The child's language was aggressive and full of expletives when he was angry. The other pupils were at about level two or three in English; they could just write a story with some support. All the children in the class were lively and the form tutor had told the teacher that the pupils enjoyed their music and drama lessons.

Behaviour management was a key concern for the teacher in every lesson which had to have a very clear structure to engage the group and keep them on task. In each lesson the names of the pupils who got started quickly were listed on the left-hand side of the board. Key words were listed and used to teach spelling and vocabulary. Learning aims were simple, clearly displayed and clearly explained. Good handwriting and neat, decorated work was valued. At the end of the lesson, if pupils were participating and listening well during the summation, extra ticks would be added above names. The emphasis was always on the positive and the teacher would give three clear warnings before a child was given any kind of punishment, e.g. a letter home, a withdrawal of a privilege or a detention. Complete refusal to cooperate or abusive behaviour meant that pupils would be removed from the classroom through the faculty rota system. This system allowed teachers to nominate their most reasonable lessons for a slot where they could receive pupils who needed to be removed from other classes. Being able to remove a child, when you absolutely have to, is an absolutely essential feature of being able to manage such turbulent classes. The pupil most likely to leave the room was the white pupil described above.

The teacher also gave the week's lessons a clear structure linked into a class rewards system. For example, on Fridays, after homework, often reading and spelling, had been checked, the pupils who had completed homework and behaved well that week were rewarded with a smiley face merit stamp. They would then be allowed to go to the library for reading and research. These library lessons were very popular because the library was a very attractive space and the pupils enjoyed the prepared treasure-hunt-type tasks around key topics, using novels and non-fiction, dictionaries, thesauri and encyclopedias. The pupils who had misbehaved would be held back as a punishment while the TA took the other children with her. During another term the Friday reward was a visit to the ICT suite. The TA was happy with the way her time was used and worked well with the teacher. At the end of each half-term there would be edible prizes and certificates for the pupils.

After establishing some kind of basic routine it became possible to be a little more adventurous with this group and establish pair work, e.g. stick and paste or sequencing activities, as part of the lesson. To begin a unit on non-fiction writing the teacher decided to teach the pupils how to give instructions. The lesson had been tried out successfully in a higher set (see Figure 7.1) and now it was the turn of this group to try out the exercise.

The group was told the aims of the lesson – to learn how to give instructions and use language clearly and precisely. The teacher, very demonstratively, told the pupils to come into the room, to sit down quickly and quietly and record the aims of the lesson in their books. After the pupils had done this they were asked if they could remember the instructions they had been given. The pupils quickly identified the instructions and the teacher discussed the meaning of the word instruction, the context in which instructions were used, how they should be used, the choice of words, tone of voice and the body language required to give instructions.

The teacher then told the class they were going to play the 'Alien Coat Game'. A coat was placed on a chair and the teacher asked for an assistant. Several hands went up as the class was fully engaged. The teacher chose one child who had completed writing the aims and key words and the teacher sent this child out of the room, giving him a brief explanation of his role. He was to act the role of the alien who did not understand the meaning of the word coat. By this time all the pupils had written out

Subject: Teacher:	Topic: The Alien Coat Game	Form: Date: Monday 14th Feb

Learning Objectives
• To understand the importance of clear instructions.
• To learn how to use language precisely.

Main teaching points/activities (timed)
• Lesson objectives – homework?
• Teacher explains what an instruction is. Emphasises the imperative (sentence level).
• Teacher demonstrates the game with pupil as the alien.
• Check that pupils are clear about what they have to do in pairs in playing the game –
  one alien/one gives instructions.
Plenary: demonstration? Which instructions worked? Why?

Homework (set at beginning of lesson)
• Highlight discourse markers (word level).
• Check HWK days.
• For example: write a recipe for a meal of your choice.

Materials
• Boardmarker, merit stamp, pupils and a coat.

Key words
• Instruction; precise; imperative; discourse markers.

Assessment (if applicable)
• Rewards if HWK Diary or similar available.
• Plenary checks learning objectives.
• Pair work could be used for En1 assessment.

What next?
• To read and evaluate a text giving instructions in terms of organisation and layout.

Figure 7.1 Lesson plan.

their aims and were ready to play the game. Allowing pupils enough
time to complete each task is a very important part of managing a group
like this.

The teacher asked the pupil to enter the room and told the children
that an alien had arrived from outer space who did not know what a coat
was. The teacher then modelled a series of very precise instructions to
tell the alien how to put the coat on:

• Walk forward to that corner of the room and then stop
• Now turn around and walk towards the desk

- Place your hand on the soft, blue object hanging on the back of the chair. . . .

She then asked two pupils to come and model the exercise. They started to do this but to the great delight of the class the alien became far less passive and obedient. It adopted a series of dalek like murmurs and began to clink and clank. The alien had immediately developed a far stronger identity than in the higher set. The pupils were now begging the teacher to allow every child in the room to have a public perform-ance as the alien. It was becoming very difficult to get them to play the role of the instructor!

Eventually the teacher persuaded them to practise the exercise in pairs, as she had planned, and then quite a few were able to perform their improvisation at the end of the lesson. The most challenging child, whose behaviour patterns were described earlier, gave the star turn as the funniest alien of all. A teaching moment, or mini-plenary as the text-books now call it, took place to deconstruct the language features of the instructions by asking which instructions worked best and why.

This moment was brief, however, as the clamour in the classroom was from pupils wanting to enact the game in front of their peers. Pressure was then placed on the teacher to allow the pupils to write this up as a play. Surprised and pleased that the pupils were demanding to write something down, the teacher promised that this would happen in the next lesson. The pupils had not only upstaged the top set and flung themselves wholeheartedly into the drama activity but had then sug-gested their own extension activity, which involved drafting a script.

Why did this group of pupils show such enthusiasm for this particular exercise? Perhaps one of the answers lies in the identification with the alien. Here was a chance to perform and be foolish, naughty and dumb and be allowed to get away with it. The dumber the alien, the more the class laughed. The more peculiar the alien's characteristics, the greater the kudos of the actor for his performance. Some of the energy usually directed towards misbehaving could be channelled into this task.

The exercise allowed pupils to be orally inventive with language, to use their imagination and their performance skills. Drama is both a kin-aesthetic and a use-of-language activity. It allows for movement, gesture, parody and use of classroom space. This activity freed up the minds of pupils often overburdened with the obstacles that reading and writing present to them. But, as good teaching should not just stay in the com-fort zone, the extension activity challenged them to use the versatility of their oral language to produce some inventive written language. They had to work hard to reproduce the speech and sounds of the alien. They wanted to write the speech down because they wanted to capture the activity and re-read it. The teacher had to teach the class how to write dialogue and stage directions in the next lesson. She also had to write down some of the alien sounds for them to use. The desire to read it aloud was another conquest because this had now become a reading activity too. The pupils felt in control of their learning. The 'aliens' in the class had found a route out of the normally alienating experience of school.

The activity was also modelled and they were given a chance to practise and perfect the exercise. The oral rehearsal meant that when it came to writing they were confident about what they wanted to write about. Writing in partners meant that they were helping and prompting each other and this peer scaffolding gave them added support.

Thus we can see that children with SEN, and in this particular case study the School Action Plus child, can be motivated to learn through talk and drama and through working collaboratively. If the exercise is clearly modelled or explained, has relevance and a purpose, if it appeals to their imagination, their inner experience, if it draws on the skills they already have and refines and develops them, talk-based lessons can be successful. The pupils realise that they can achieve with you and that you are someone who will help them to learn. After these lessons trust between the pupils and the teacher grew and the teacher became more relaxed and at ease with the class. But each lesson still had to be very carefully prepared and, even then, could still sometimes go wrong.

Key Points: Special Needs and talk

- Make sure you are aware which pupils have SEN
- Have clear structures, rules and routines for your lessons
- Make it very clear what you want the pupils to do at each stage
- Work with the teaching assistant to allocate clear roles for each adult
- Model the task where appropriate and list and explain key words
- Allow pupils time to complete work and to practise activities
- Train pupils to listen and to read and write collaboratively
- Choose talk tasks that build on existing skills/knowledge
- Choose talk tasks that engage the pupils' imagination
- Be flexible, stay relaxed and use humour to lighten the load
- Use rewards frequently and fairly and keep building the relationship with pupils.

Chapter 8

Gender and talk

Boys are four times more likely to join in discussion, make comments in class.

Stanworth (1987)

Many government reports about boys' underachievement in English have focused on the lower attainment of boys in examinations. There are undoubtedly differences between boys' and girls' development and progress in reading and writing. However, as others have pointed out, the differences between the performance in English of boys from different socioeconomic groups are greater than the differences between boys and girls. This suggests that there is sometimes an oversimplification of the debate about gender and achievement in English and that it is not all boys who are underachieving but particularly those in lower socioeconomic groups.

When it comes to speaking and listening the gender issues are complex and do not seem to follow the patterns suggested for reading and writing. There has been less debate in government reports on differences in the achievement of boys and girls in speaking and listening. Here again we confront the problem that public exams before age 16 do not assess speaking and listening. Although the GCSE English exam allocates 20 per cent of the final marks for speaking and listening, this is no longer listed as a separate grade. It is thus difficult to collect evidence about gender and talk from English examination results. It might be pertinent to ask whether the bias towards reading and writing in the SATS at 7, 11 and 14 actually serves to depress boys' attainment in English as this is an area where, at the end of Key Stage 4 for example, many boys appear to do well.

Earlier work by feminist researchers and those working in the National Oracy project did point to some differences between boys and girls in their attitude to class discussion and work in small groups. There is some recognition of this work on gender socialisation in the QCA handbook (DFES, 2003e) on *Speaking, Listening and Learning in Key Stages 1 and 2*: 'Girls are generally more collaborative, supporting each other and developing ideas together. Boys often like to propose ideas, to use language dramatically and to move on fast rather than develop detail.'

In this chapter we will look at the role of the teacher in supporting both girls and boys in different talk-based tasks.

The girls?

Feminist researchers such as Firth (1987) have investigated the equal opportunity issues for girls in schools. Stanworth (1987), looking at pupil reports of classroom interaction, suggested that boys

> were four times more likely to join in discussion or to offer comments in class. They are twice as likely to demand help or attention from the teacher . . . More importantly, it seems to pupils that boys receive the lion's share of teacher's attention and regard.

Crawford (1995) has also highlighted the ways in which boys can dominate in whole class settings and even in pair or small group work.

It might be necessary to allocate the role of chair and other roles carefully, as suggested in Chapter 4, to ensure that girls do not always end up as the scribes. A dominant character might be allocated the role of chair or an object can be used to pass around and encourage turn taking. Alternatively, a talk frame can be provided to help all pupils access the task.

The teacher will also need to decide on group composition and vary the gender composition of groupings: sometimes mixed, sometimes all girls and all boys, sometimes friendship groups. Classes that are familiar with group work will accept this and reflections on the task will help pupils understand the benefits of working in different groups. The teacher will want to explain the choice of grouping at some point in the discussion so that pupils understand the decisions made and how they are linked to learning. Teachers need to ensure that assessment takes place in a variety of contexts to ensure that girls' skills are not undervalued, as they often make particularly insightful contributions when working with their peers.

The *Macbeth* casting activity, outlined in Chapter 4 on group work, is a sustained oral assignment that is a good example of an activity that is highly appropriate for a mixed setting. It involved two Jigsaws that allowed groups of male and female pupils, in their specialist groups, to discuss the characteristics of a particular character in *Macbeth* and then join together in home groups to provide a job description for the actors they would want in several different roles. In the second session the groups made their choices in their home groups and then had to argue their case for the choices they had made in a whole class session. This is where the teacher would have to be aware of the problems of boys potentially dominating and ensure that some kind of gender balance was maintained by choosing to ask an appropriate number of female and male pupils for their opinions. The teacher might also need to insist that all contributions were carefully listened to.

Preparation of whole class discussion and presentations becomes an even more important feature if teachers wish to encourage girls to play an equal public role in classroom discourse. Girls still do not have as many natural role models as boys for public discourse, for many of these roles in the real world are still dominated by men. It may be necessary to balance or structure presentations to encourage more equal gender representation.

In Chapter 9 on pupils evaluating talk we build on what has already been said about how to question and structure report backs. Among social constructivists there has been an ongoing discussion about how to encourage a real debate on the process of learning through small group talk. In *Culture and Pedagogy*, R. Alexander (2000) comments on the quality of talk in primary classrooms in different countries. He questions the aim of always trying to involve every pupil in a discussion and suggests that one sustained, reflective contribution can be perhaps more important for learning than shorter, possibly more superficial, contributions from a large number of pupils. Teachers should ensure that they encourage boys and girls to make those sustained, reflective contributions.

In another session it may be appropriate for a larger number of pupils to contribute at the end in, for example, a more open-ended discussion. Such a session would be prompted by open-ended questions that the teacher might need to plan for. Which ever form is appropriate for the plenary, the teacher should be conscious of the roles boys and girls are playing. An awareness of the ways in which gender roles can influence talk in whole class and group discussion will thus ensure that all pupils gain from all forms of group work and classroom talk. In lower sets, in challenging groups, where there are sometimes only a few girls, the teacher needs to be particularly aware of these issues.

Key points for involving girls in speaking and listening activities:

- Plan for small group exploratory and collaborative talk and monitor what is happening within the groups by, for example, observing one mixed-gender group closely.
- Train the pupils in active listening to all pupils in the class.
- Ascribe roles when you feel it is appropriate to do so.
- Vary the groupings to allow pupils to work in friendship groups, including single-gender groups, and groups that you establish.
- Be prepared to take positive action to involve girls in chairing discussions, performance, group and individual presentations if necessary.
- Try to give pupils choices over topics for talk and ensure that you cater for both genders.

The boys

There can be no doubt that boys enjoy lessons based on talk, including structured small group talk that involves problem solving, drama and purposeful whole class discussion. A one-to-one discussion with the teacher also works well with boys. In fact lessons that have no writing in them, or a series of lessons that have little writing in them, can have a highly motivating effect on boys. As with all pupils, if you give them something they can do, they really begin to fly.

However, the structure, and therefore the planning, has to be very tight for male pupils. Particularly in all-male settings, they will ride rough-shod over any lesson that is poorly planned with unclear out-comes. Teachers need to make their explanations clear and concise in explaining what the pupils have to do, how and why they have to do it. The group activity must be a task that requires a decision and a solution. Boys will undermine any aspect of a task that is not really necessary. A summary at the end is also important.

Many of the tasks described in this book have worked successfully in boys' schools, but there are some that stand out. As outlined in Chapter 5, one-minute storytelling caused a fantastic buzz in two different Key

Stage 4 classes of boys. Media simulations, whether making a presentation of their ideas for a new situation comedy or producing their own local radio news programme, were also memorable moments when the pupils were able to use their own cultural capital to produce a media text. Quizzes, word and spelling games are particularly popular, even with boys with low levels of literacy, because they revise and sum up learning and break it down into chunks and events.

Prizes, distributed widely, add to momentum and the lower the ability of the group, the larger the number of rewards should be. Drama also gives a secure structure for boys to experiment with language and play reading is particularly popular. Boys will often be happy to take on female roles, particularly in all-boy settings, in order to read aloud.

Boys enjoy reading as well as just talking: sometimes when reading, drama or speaking and listening is the outcome of the lesson boys will sit up and pay attention. They feel that this is something they will be able to do. The oral component in assessment for GCSE English literature, which is discussed in Chapter 10, builds on the skills of oral intelligence and is a very popular and well-used form of assessment in many boys' schools.

The most naughty, non-conformist boys are often among the most intelligent students and a lot of the intellectual energy of adolescent boys is directed at making lessons fun by off-task behaviour. This is the case to some degree with all pupils when the lesson fails to engage. Clowning around becomes an art form in itself in this kind of lesson. Even when engaged, many boys will still clown around but it will be easier to redirect the pupil if most pupils are really involved in the lesson.

The teacher has to catch boys being good and make them show you what they can do. One of the greatest paradoxes of boys is that the emotional engagement with the lesson and the teacher is of paramount importance. The teacher can be male or female but you have to be prepared, at some level, to make learning fun and be able to adapt to the pupils' moods. If you can use humour to quell or redirect misbehaviour, without humiliating the pupil, you will often start to win the class over. You must be in charge, but you must also be flexible to allow for pupil response.

Key points for involving boys in speaking and listening activities:

- Make sure your planning is very tight and that the lesson requires group work.
- Establish very clear aims and ground rules, e.g. insist that your cueing system is respected.
- Give clear, specific instructions about, for example, the task and the groupings.
- Break up the learning when it is appropriate to do so. Plan to revise and summarise at key points.
- Allow pupils to evaluate the progress they are making in speaking and listening and discuss how this contributes to other learning inside and outside school.
- Use praise, one-to-one sometimes, and humour, where appropriate.

Many of these points are obviously transferable between boys and girls but gender socialisation is part of the hidden curriculum. Pupils come into classrooms with assumptions about gender roles, imposed on them from wider society. Speaking and listening activities can serve to reinforce inequality if the teacher does not have an awareness of gender equality issues.

Chapter 9

Pupils evaluating talk

I enjoyed the oral assignment because I think I'm at my best when I have to perform in front of an audience.

Year 10 pupil

Assessment involves judging pupils against specific criteria for speaking and listening. Evaluation is the process that the student and the teacher should go through to judge the quality of the learning and teaching that has taken place. The stage of reflection and evaluation helps students become better learners and allows the teacher to improve their teaching. Students learn how to analyse their strengths and weaknesses as learners. Evaluation is a crucial part of the ongoing cycle of planning, teaching, monitoring and reviewing practice. Reflective teachers, who want to promote collaborative talk, ask questions such as:

- What exactly did the students learn?
- Was the task too difficult or too easy?
- Were the instructions clear?
- Did the pupils have the skills to collaborate effectively?
- Did the class know why they were working in groups?
- Has there been too much group work?

Ask the pupils?

Reflective teachers pose these kinds of questions at the end of their lessons. Pupil evaluations help the teacher to really know what their pupils think. In fact some of the questions you might ask yourself at the end of an oral lesson, or series of lessons, can also be put to the pupils. The discussion will be a good one, because you really want to know the answers. You may wish to carry out evaluations with a small group or with the whole class.

As oral assignments and evaluations become a regular feature of classroom practice the pupils will become more sophisticated in their judgements of, for example, small group discussion. They will also become more aware of the needs of an audience when performing, reading aloud, giving presentations, and more conscious of different techniques that a speaker can use to keep the attention of their audience.

Many students, from different backgrounds, acquire these skills through reading and discussion at home or through readings and performance in religious settings and they simply need to be developed. But many socially disadvantaged students or students new to English need the skills of careful listening and sharing ideas, discussion and presentation of ideas, and the appropriate use of formal language to be more explicitly taught. This requires teacher and pupil modelling and the creation of clear structures and routines for group work.

The role oral evaluation plays in learning

Oral evaluations, as a group or as individuals, raise the status and prestige of oral work in the classroom and therefore encourage pupils to value their spoken language and their ability to talk in a range of contexts. As pupils gain an understanding of the importance of speaking and listening they also begin to appreciate the role it can play in enriching their experience of reading and helping them improve the quality and range of their writing. The metalanguage, the language they use to talk about how to talk in differing contexts, gives them greater control over language choices and the beginning of an understanding that there is a grammar of talk and that grammar is not just for reading and writing. Careful reflection on what has been achieved after some of the exercises outlined in earlier chapters therefore reinforces the learning and helps to increase the self-esteem of all pupils.

Oral evaluation is only one form of pupil self-assessment and is therefore linked to formative assessment, assessment for learning, giving pupils very specific advice on how to improve. The principle of self-assessment can also be applied to reading and writing and all forms of learning. As this book is focused on talk, it will concentrate on the evaluation of talk.

One of the reasons why pupil evaluation of talk is particularly useful is because of the nature of talk and the difficulty the teacher faces in keeping evidence of talk and making judgements about talk. Talk is transient, spontaneous and has to be evaluated and assessed as it takes place. For the busy English teacher, who is always under pressure to mark written work and to deliver levels of pupil attainment, it is very easy not to prioritise either evaluation or assessment of talk. Systems of evidence collection and evaluation therefore have to be simple and user-friendly to be of actual use in the classroom. Once again the often excellent advice in textbooks and government documents can be far too cumbersome for the overburdened classroom teacher.

One of the advantages of pupil oral evaluation is that, to some extent, the pupils are commenting on or recording their own oral work for the teacher. This means that some of the process of collecting evidence is devolved and the teacher's time can be used more effectively for making the judgements when it is necessary to do so. It is also a more qualitative form of evidence collection, focusing on the process of learning, and thus it avoids simply putting pupils in a level 2a, 2c or 5b slot.

This stage is therefore an important one and needs to be a planned part of the teaching for a particular text or topic. The system suggested here, of a group or individual record kept by the pupils, provides an excellent written record or diary of evidence for the whole class. Pupils can keep these sheets in their English folders (see Figure 9.1) which the teacher can use to assist in any report writing or summative assessment.

Date	A Record of My Oral Work – Year 10
23/3/02	We performed a scene called the psychiatrist's couch. I played the role of Iago who answered questions put by G who played the psychiatrist. I enjoyed this role because it allowed me to create a scenario outside the boundaries set by Shakespeare. Our presentation was successful because of our original view of Iago's background. We came up with viable explanations to partly explain Iago's alternative behaviour. We could have improved by presenting a more thoroughly researched view that was likely to occur in those times.
Task: Drama	Reading and performing key scenes of Othello after watching John Othello. This pair of students chose an improvisation that explored Iago's personality.

Figure 9.1 Oral record completed by pupil.

Evaluating roles

If the teacher has decided to give pupils roles in the group, e.g. chair, scribe, reporter, the groups can then be reorganised to reflect together on how well they fulfilled their roles and how they might improve. The teacher would ask the pupils to work in groups with other chairs, scribes, etc. to discuss this and report back. Organising the process of reflection like this will prepare a good classroom discussion in which children have already articulated and rehearsed their thoughts. This can also be achieved with other forms of role play.

Evaluating group discussion

This requires the group to discuss how well they worked and to write up a group report reflecting on what they have done and how well they worked together. For example:

- Why did the group work well together?
- What did you have to do to be able to complete the task?
- What did not work?

Or you might wish to focus on more specific skills such as giving reasons for opinions, building on each other's points, using the ground rules suggested below.

Ground rules

Ground rules for talk, recently advocated by Neil Mercer (2000), can help a class evaluate talk. The class can be asked to discuss what conditions they would like to see for work in small groups. They may come up with ideas such as:

- Sit so that everyone can see each other
- Listen carefully to each other
- Allow the chair to choose people to speak
- Avoid shouting out and disturbing other groups
- Give reasons for your arguments.

Individual groups can then use this as a checklist to see whether they followed these or another set of rules. The class may decide to add to or change the ground rules as a result of the evaluation or they may decide to continue to use those rules. This and similar checklists make it clear exactly what you want the children to do.

Whole class evaluation

When a particular task has been completed and some kind of presentation delivered, the class could discuss the positive features of the task or presentation and consider how it could be made even better. The class can discuss any stage of the process – how they became engaged, how the groups worked, whether the presentations were effective – but the class needs to be trained in this practice of reflection. We have already suggested a number of methods that the teacher can use to structure these sessions:

- Make the purpose of the discussion clear at the outset, including the need for active listening
- Manage feedback so that pupils learn something new, asking one group to feed back and asking others to make comparisons
- Discuss the characteristics of effective group work
- Use adult/student observers of particular groups or the whole class to feed back
- Use the 'join up with another group' approach or 'envoys' where one individual is sent to another group to find out what they have been doing and then report back
- Sit in a circle where all have eye contact, are encouraged to name other participants and build on each other's points for more reflective discussions
- Perhaps use a semi-circle where classroom layout makes the circle too difficult an arrangement
- The goldfish bowl strategy where one group rehearses their discussion in the midst of the group while others listen and make comments at the end
- Open questioning techniques which both teacher and students are allowed to use
- Wait time and thinking time which can lead to more thoughtful discussion.

At first, when pupils are commenting on others' work it may be appropriate to allow only positive comments. But as pupils become more familiar and comfortable with speaking to the whole group, the teacher could introduce the idea of at least three positive remarks before pupils are allowed to make a criticism. The teacher can then lead a summary discussion, asking the question 'How might we do it differently next time?' This could lead to the class providing a list of specific pieces of advice about how to improve for the next time. This process trains the pupils to positively evaluate the work of a group, the work of the whole class and the contribution of individuals. It reinforces the idea that we are all learning together.

A record of my oral work

Individual pupil records (see Figure 9.2) allow each pupil to describe their work and to reflect on their role in the group. They may need to be used with an aide-mémoire to prompt the pupil's reflections. Such an aide-mémoire can be designed by the teacher for a particular task and written on the whiteboard or prepared in advance.

Some suggestions for an aide-mémoire might be:

I worked with _____

Our task was to _____

I learnt that _____

I played the role/helped the group by _____

We worked quite/very well because _____

The difficulties we overcame were _____

We could have improved by _____

I could have improved by _____

I enjoyed/did not enjoy this task because _____

Other comments. _____

These are simple prompts which some children may need to get started on an evaluation. Others will be able to write their own account and should be encouraged to add their own reflections as they wish. This is only an example; the teacher may want to focus on more specific skills, or, alternatively, use a 'talk journal' in a more open-ended way, like a reading journal, where pupils make comments on how they felt about a particular activity. The oral record or journal provides a structure for pupils' thinking about group learning and pupils of all abilities can attempt an evaluation in this form. The prompts can be shortened or read aloud to EAL pupils very new to English.

| Name: | | | Class: | | | |

Date	Comments	Whole class	Small group	Pair work	Indi- vidual
	Student's signature:				
	Leave this box blank, in case your teacher wants to make a comment:				

Figure 9.2 Oral work record sheet.

Using tape recorders or dictaphones

This involves a small group working independently in a quiet corner or outside the classroom while the tape recorder records the discussion. Recording group discussions and possibly using them in future lessons will show the pupils that you value their discussion and that it contributes to everyone's learning. Nearly all the group activities suggested can be recorded which immediately makes evaluation much easier for pupils and teachers.

Oral diary

This is a different approach which can be set as homework or as an extension exercise for pupils who like a challenge. The pupils have to record the opportunities for talk and discussion in all their lessons as if they were writing a diary for a week, and try to reflect on the purpose and value of talk in assisting learning. This is really a piece of action research by pupils.

Once the pupils have recorded each lesson for one week the teacher may wish to photocopy the pages and ask the pupils to discuss their findings as a class or as a separate group if it has been an extension task. Some suggestions for questions might be:

- What is the most common form of talk in class?
- How often each week do you work in groups?
- When you worked in groups did you work well together?
- What do you feel the pupils learnt from working in groups?
- What kind of class discussion took place in different lessons?
- How would you describe the type of language the teacher was using?
- How would you describe the language of the pupils?
- Are there any other patterns you can establish?
- How do you think speaking and listening and talk in small groups contributes to your learning?
- Are there any problems with this type of learning?
- Any other comments?

The discussion that ensues can be a whole class or an independent group conversation recorded on tape. The children are evaluating the process of learning in school in some detail and you will gain valuable insights into teaching and learning across the curriculum from such an activity.

Records for GCSE English

Pupil evaluations also provide a record of the assignments for En 1 (Speaking and Listening) for GCSE. They will aid you in completing the summative assessment forms for individual and group work and for drama which are included in coursework folders at the end of Key Stage 4. You will have a detailed description of the task and a record of the role the pupil played in each oral assignment. If the sheets are kept in the coursework folders, alongside the written coursework, they will not be mislaid. Such folders provide impressive evidence for observations by inspectors.

The evaluations encourage pupils to be independent and to take responsibility for improving their own learning. They will also provide you with instant feedback which allows you to discuss, reflect on and adapt your teaching to respond to the pupils' needs and concerns.

Chapter 10

Teachers assessing talk

> The curricular and social demands of 2015 are likely to include evidence of collaborative working as well as individual working. . . . Drama, speaking and listening should be foregrounded as a key mode of teaching and assessment not in English alone but also across the curriculum.
>
> NATE (2005)

Of all the challenges involved in using talk in the classroom, the task of assessing talk often poses teachers the greatest challenge. There are many reasons for this.

The first is the debate among teachers about whether talk should be assessed. Some of those who have promoted the debate on the use of small group learning believe that talk is intrinsic to learning and can be evaluated but should not form the basis for summative assessment. Exploratory talk is by its nature tentative and should be leading to greater clarity or understanding. It is not necessarily appropriate for an exploratory discussion to be observed or assessed. Indeed, in many cases any form of assessment might inhibit the discussion. Presentations by pupils demonstrate outcomes but they, again, do not need to be assessed in order to be valued by the students. Many might argue that teachers need to consider carefully whether assessment is required and when it is required to focus on formative judgements that help students identify areas for improvement.

The teacher can ensure progress in speaking and listening by:

- creating a wide range of contexts for talk, to different classes, both in and outside the school
- encouraging a variety of opportunities for talk, e.g. talking about

direct experience, whole class discussion and debate, small group talk, performance and presentation and reflective discussion

- encouraging pupil evaluation by making expectations clear and allowing pupils to judge how well they have done through the use of recording, oral records or logs, pupil and adult observers, discussing talk tasks and setting their own targets as discussed in Chapter 9
- helping pupils sustain their talk by planning for extended assignments over two or three lessons, e.g. Jigsaw (Chapter 4), moving from twos to fours, modelling, planning and rehearsing talk, as suggested in the cascade storytelling exercise (Chapter 5), and questioning pupils sensitively, as suggested in Chapter 2.

On the other hand, the requirement to complete summative assessments of pupil attainment in Speaking and Listening at GCSE level has embedded this strand more strongly in schemes of work at Key Stage 4 than at any other stage of pupils' learning. The requirement for a final grade, with evidence of assessment, and the training that accompanied the introduction of this new form of assessment, has allowed teachers and departments to plan for extended oral assignments and pupil evaluation as part of their GCSE courses. In challenging classrooms this has helped to motivate a wider range of students (Coultas, 2006b) and assisted pupils in preparing for oral assessments for GCSE English literature coursework. The assessment cycle planned over the two years should be formative because at each point the teacher can encourage pupils to identify their own strengths and areas for improvement.

Many teachers are, however, less familiar and confident with this mode of assessment. As argued in previous chapters, the general effect of the SATS has been to take teachers away from planning and creating opportunities to assess talk. In all the earlier key stages, teacher assessment of speaking and listening is encouraged but it has little significance in the summative assessment. The SATS, as written tests, have reinforced a hierarchy in English teaching that places writing and reading (reading is judged primarily through written responses) at the top of the scale and speaking and listening much lower down.

Although more recent documentation from QCA (2003) urges primary school teachers to plan for speaking and listening and drama, the National Literacy Strategy in Primary Schools initially gave teachers little advice about speaking and listening, drama and media education. As discussed earlier, teachers, and head teachers in particular, are sent very forceful messages about what is important in these exams.

It is also difficult to assess talk, particularly if you have had little training and practice. Talk is transient, as mentioned previously, but it is also particularly open to subjective judgements as we may respond positively or negatively to tone of voice, accent and mannerisms in speech. We have to be very careful to use criteria-referenced judgements when assessing talk. The advice here on assessment is the same as in the rest of the book: start small, make it simple, user-friendly and link it to the learning.

Formative and summative assessment

The distinction between formative and summative is important in all forms of assessment, but especially so in the assessment of speaking and listening. Formative assessment is work in progress, describing and commenting on how the child is developing and how they can move forward. Summative assessment states how far the child has reached in a particular stage. It is a snapshot of their development.

The vast majority of assessment of speaking and listening should be formative, celebrating what a child can do and suggesting how they can build on this. This will not involve ascribing grades or levels but simply means the teacher describes how well the child has done in the particular task and offers some suggestions for improvement. The research carried out on 'Assessment for Learning' has proved that formative assessment can have a very important impact on children's learning. An approach that identifies strengths and builds on these to set targets is particularly important with speaking and listening. Our speech is closely linked to our culture and our identity.

Formative assessment

Pupil evaluation

If you have already begun to carry out pupil evaluations, then you have already begun assessment for learning. These take you in the right direction and show that you are recording what you are doing by delineating and evaluating teaching sessions based on talk and giving pupils formative advice about how to improve their oral skills. For many oral exercises you may decide to choose this form of self-assessment.

Who answers questions?

Questioning as a method of checking learning was discussed in Chapter 2. You are already assessing understanding through class discussion and questioning and when pupils answer, you are often assessing talk. The teacher acts as a role model for talk. As you make statements and answer pupils' questions, as you talk to other members of staff, the children are watching you and unconsciously learning how to talk. Make sure you are always polite to other adults because the children will notice if you are not! Sometimes you will rephrase an answer, or sum up their point, thus modelling how to answer the question, how to construct a clear sentence in speech. You should avoid doing this too often or you will suppress meaningful dialogue but sometimes it is appropriate to do so.

You might then move from these question-and-answer sessions, something you do naturally, to monitoring and assessing who listens and speaks well in class. You are generally aware of who speaks a lot in class but you can approach this more systematically by having an observer, a pupil, a teaching assistant (TA) or a learning support teacher (LST) watch the class. This is a very good way of making students (and teachers) accountable for listening and speaking and developing these skills.

- Get a pupil or a TA/LST to act as an observer
- Tell the class that the observer has a grid or tally to check who is listening and who is contributing
- Give the observer a list of names and ask them to mark out who listens well, who listens very well, who contributes and who makes a particularly good contribution
- Get the observer or TA/LST to report back to the class and get them to suggest who should have the rewards for that lesson.

This is excellent practice for team teaching and really uses the extra adult in the room effectively. It can take place at the beginning or end of the lesson, or at any point when you have a sustained interaction with the whole class. If a child is carrying out the role they will usually be very enthusiastic and fair towards other children if you have explained clearly what they have to do. You can then discuss the information with the pupils and take steps to ensure that all children have a chance to make contributions by planning for different opportunities for talk and ensuring that your questioning and prompts extend their thinking.

Creating assessment moments

The teacher has to plan for moments of assessment. Speaking and listening tasks should be included in every scheme of work and medium-term plan. Most lessons should allow some opportunity for pupils to collaborate with their peers, even if it is only for a short period. But not every speaking and listening activity has to be assessed. As speaking and listening feeds into every aspect of learning, it should enrich the experience of reading and writing. It is only necessary to assess how pupils talk at particular moments when you decide you need to.

It is normal practice for a formative assessment opportunity to be created once a term at Key Stages 2 and 3. At Key Stage 4 you may wish to have them twice a term to ensure that you cover the tasks required in the syllabus to prepare for a summative assessment in En 1. In fact, English teams and departments that plan for sustained oral assignments for each unit of work provide an enriched curriculum (Coultas, 2006b). Boys are often particularly motivated by the instant feedback such assessment occasions provide.

Creating an assessment moment means telling the class how they will be assessed for that lesson, group discussion, presentation, individual talk or drama performance. You may wish to create some clear criteria yourself, or with colleagues engaged in the same assignment, which you share with the pupils. You can give verbal or written feedback in their books or on their oral records. If you are eventually going to ascribe levels or grades, you may wish older children to see the En 1 level descriptors so they know how they are being judged (see Figure 10.3). These assessment moments act as a focus for the pupils and often make turbulent classes behave better.

It is good practice for English departments and literacy coordinators to plan for these assessment moments in schemes of work and medium-term plans by giving teachers some suggestions from which they can choose.

Observation

The close observation of one pupil or group of pupils can reveal important insights into children's oral abilities. The teacher or adult can sit beside the group and observe the discussion, recording who is contributing and the roles pupils are playing, and how the group is working together. The recording needs to be as objective as possible. The teacher can report back to the group at the end of the discussion and use these insights to develop oral skills and guide future teaching plans.

The Richmond English Record (see Figure 10.1) is a useful grid for analysing the higher-order skills that pupils are using and gives the teacher an opportunity to record the group response. Notes on observations can be kept in an exercise book or a file with dates; this will be useful to refer back to when writing up reports in the same way as pupils' oral evaluations can assist this process.

An aide-mémoire of things to look for (tick those features observed)

Look for signs of
evaluative and
reflective thinking:

questioning commenting repeating participating describing responding reinforcing suggesting . . .	**Name:** **Date:** **Activity:** Size of group: Record of observation:	supporting asserting planning collaborating initiating narrating sequencing stating . . .
arguing discussing requesting reasoning persuading conceding encouraging . . .		speculating hypothesising negotiating justifying categorising recalling comparing . . .
reflecting . . .	(Initials)	

Look for communication strategies:

listening attentively	facial expressions
body language	awareness of audience
gestures	bludgeoning
eye contact	causing silences
	. . .

Figure 10.1 Speaking and listening observation sheet.
Source: The Richmond English Record (1989).

The teacher can only observe one group like this per lesson and you will have to plan carefully when you do it in challenging classrooms. You need to be sure that the other groups are really engaged with their task while you observe and plan for each group to be observed for a period of, say, 10–15 minutes. It is preferable to do this when another adult is working with you but that cannot always be arranged.

This observation method is therefore useful for formative assessment. After looking at the notes, the teacher would need to rank the pupils and then ascribe levels if using observations for summative assessments.

Towards summative assessment

An overall framework – ranking

When you do have to allocate a level, as at GCSE, an overall approach is needed in understanding how to make fair judgements of pupils' oral skills. Pupils will do better at some tasks than others and you will want to give a range of assessments and then decide on a final grade.

The best method is to start by ranking the children in a particular exercise. Observing a group discussion, for example, where children give a short talk on a topic of their choice would be a good place to start. You can then follow these steps:

- You decide which talk was most effective in capturing and sustaining the interest of the audience. You may find you think that two pupils did this best.
- You then choose the pupils who were close to this standard and then again at the next level. You may find that more than one talk has been quite effective for different reasons.
- You then look at the National Curriculum level descriptors (see Figure 10.2) or GCSE level descriptors (see Figure 10.3) for En 1, Speaking and Listening, and decide where you would place the most effective talk. You match the skills demonstrated to the overall characteristics of the descriptor.
- You then look at the next level of students and see where they fit. It may be that they have reached a particular level but that they are less secure in it. Then you can use your level 4a, 4b and 4c to make a smaller distinction between them as you would when marking a piece of writing. The layout of the boxes helps you to do this.

Key Stage 2 and 3 assessment	
KS2 Class: 4 5 6 KS3 Form: 7 8 9 Name: En 1 – Speaking and listening	
Level 1 Pupils talk about matters of immediate interest. They listen to others and usually respond appropriately. They convey simple meanings to a range of listeners, speaking audibly, and begin to extend their ideas or accounts by providing some detail.	
Level 2 Pupils begin to show confidence in talking and listening, particularly where the topics interest them. On occasions, they show awareness of the needs of the listener by including relevant detail. In developing and explaining their ideas they speak clearly and use a growing vocabulary. They usually listen carefully and respond with increasing appropriateness to what others say. They are beginning to be aware that in some situations a more formal vocabulary and tone of voice are used.	
Level 3 Pupils talk and listen confidently in different contexts, exploring and communicating ideas. In discussion, they show understanding of the main points. Through relevant comments and questions, they show they have listened carefully. They begin to adapt what they say to the needs of the listener, varying the use of vocabulary and the level of detail. They are beginning to be aware of Standard English and when it is used.	

Figure 10.2

Level 4 Pupils talk and listen with confidence in an increasing range of contexts. Their talk is adapted to the purpose: developing ideas thoughtfully, describing events and conveying their opinions clearly. In discussion, they listen carefully, making contributions and asking questions that are responsive to others' ideas and views. They use appropriately some of the features of Standard English vocabulary and grammar	
Level 5 Pupils talk and listen confidently in a wide range of contexts, including some that are of a formal nature. Their talk engages the interest of the listener as they begin to vary their expression and vocabulary. In discussion, they pay close attention to what others say, ask questions to develop ideas and make contributions that take account of others' views. They begin to use Standard English in formal situations.	
Level 6 Pupils adapt their talk to the demands of different contexts with increasing confidence. Their talk engages the interest of the listener through the variety of its vocabulary and expression. Pupils take an active part in discussion, showing understanding of ideas and sensitivity to others. They are usually fluent in their use of Standard English in formal situations.	
Level 7 Pupils are confident in matching their talk to the demands of different contexts. They use vocabulary precisely and organise their talk to communicate clearly. In discussion, pupils make significant contributions, evaluating others' ideas and varying how and when they participate. They show confident use of Standard English in situations that require it.	

Figure 10.2 continued.

Level 8 Pupils maintain and develop their talk purposefully in a range of contexts. They structure what they say clearly, using apt vocabulary and appropriate intonation and emphasis. They make a range of contributions which show that they have listened perceptively and are sensitive to the development of discussion. They show confident use of Standard English in a range of situations, adapting as necessary.	
Exceptional performance Pupils select and use structures, styles and registers appropriately in a range of contexts, varying their vocabulary and expression confidently for a range of purposes. They initiate and sustain discussion through the sensitive use of a variety of contributions. They take a leading role in discussion and listen with concentration and understanding to varied and complex speech. They show assured and fluent use of standard English in a range of situations and for a variety of purposes.	

Figure 10.2 National Curriculum speaking and listening assessment grid.

A process similar to this was the basis for moderating En 1 when it first became part of the English GCSE. The visiting moderator and the head of department would sit together and check that the correct criteria were being used to make judgements on the candidates. The teachers listening learnt a great deal about their students here. It was one of the few exam experiences that the pupils, teachers and examiners really seemed to enjoy.

This approach can be used for any individual talk, for a group discussion or performance, although it has to be adapted when assessing a whole class discussion or drama exercise which is discussed below. Once the teacher has an overall approach to assessment to guide them, they can then begin to apply and adapt this approach to particular tasks.

English – Key Stage 4 assessment Form: 10 11 Name: En 1 – Speaking and listening	
Unclassified Candidates make some attempt to speak and listen.	
Grade G Candidates speak and listen with regard to personal interests and familiar contexts. They speak audibly and listen to others, showing some recognition of the functions of Standard English.	
Grade F Candidates speak with some confidence in a range of familiar contexts, communicating clearly and adapting and organising talk to audience and purpose. They use some features of Standard English vocabulary and grammar appropriately. They listen carefully to a range of talk and respond appropriately.	
Grade E Candidates speak confidently in different contexts, showing sensitivity to situation and audience. They generally use Standard English vocabulary and grammar where appropriate. They listen with concentration to a range of talk.	
Grade D Candidates make relevant contributions to talk and are able to organise speech in collaborative contexts, varying their style of delivery as appropriate. They are increasingly aware of the need for, and use of, Standard English vocabulary and grammar. They listen carefully and make responses which show some understanding.	

Figure 10.3

Grade C Candidates speak with fluency and make significant contributions to talk in a variety of different contexts. They show a competent use of Standard English vocabulary and grammar in situations which demand it. They adapt their talk to a range of different audiences showing judgement in their choice of style and delivery to Interest listeners. They listen closely and sympathetically, responding as appropriate.	
Grade B Candidates speak purposefully in a range of contexts of increasing complexity, managing the contributions of others. They exhibit confidence and fluency in talk and show effective use of Standard English vocabulary and grammar in a range of situations. They listen with some sensitivity and respond accordingly.	
Grade A Candidates initiate speech and take a leading role in discussion, responding in detail to the ideas of others. They understand and discuss aspects of challenging content. They show an assured use of Standard English vocabulary and grammar in a range of situations and for a variety of purposes. They listen and respond to a range of complex speech.	
Grade A* Candidates show an exceptionally high ability in handling a wide range of roles. They adapt readily to task and audience, showing originality and flair where appropriate and exhibiting a depth of understanding of challenging content. They are sensitive in their choice of speech style and their use of Standard English vocabulary and grammar is mature and assured. They listen perceptively to a range of complex speech.	

Figure 10.3 GCSE speaking and listening assessment grid.

Individual presentations

The teacher needs to give a clear idea of what is expected and how the pupils will be judged. Modelling a book talk, for example, and then getting the pupils to analyse the skills involved can achieve this. You can then list these skills and attributes: clear beginnings and endings, appropriate choice of vocabulary, clear reference to genre, storyline, characters, writer's style when appropriate, ability to justify opinions, ability to hold the attention of the class.

When listening to a whole class for a formal assessment it can be useful to give the pupils an initial mark out of ten as well as writing brief comments. This is a way of ranking the whole class. You can then check the criteria for your highest mark out of ten and place the other pupils appropriately. It is very hard to make a ranking order for 25 talks over a period of lessons unless you give pupils a mark as you listen to them.

Whole class drama

When the teacher is in role as, for example, the judge in a trial, as illustrated in Chapter 6, you create a very good opportunity for assessment. But again, it is very hard to make fair judgements about the pupils when you yourself are performing a role. It is therefore necessary to sit down immediately after a lesson and give pupils a mark out of ten for their performance. You will probably remember particular roles more easily than talks in the former exercise. We have highlighted some of the references to drama in the National Curriculum (see Figure 10.4) but you might wish to use the Arts Council documentation *Drama in Schools*, that has eight level descriptors for drama, if you are particularly interested in developing pupils' skills in this area. Extended drama exercises such as this sometimes take several lessons and you can adjust the marks if you need to.

At the end of the exercise you can read the pupil oral evaluations to check your marks and then match the marks to the level descriptors as suggested previously, starting with the highest marks and deciding where they fit and then moving on down the list.

Standard English

According to Cox (1991) the only words that were deleted from the English National Curriculum document when Margaret Thatcher, then Prime Minister, looked through it were the two words 'where

Key Stage 2

En 1 Speaking and Listening

Knowledge, skills and understanding

Drama

4 To participate in a range of drama activities and to evaluate their own and others' contributions, pupils should be taught to:
   a Create, adapt and sustain different roles, individually and in groups
   b Use character, action and narrative to convey story, themes, emotions, ideas in plays they devise and script
   c Use dramatic techniques to explore characters and issues (for example, hot-seating, flashback)
   d Evaluate how they and others have contributed to the overall effectiveness of performances.

Breadth of study: Drama activities

11 The range should include:
   a improvisation and working in role
   b scripting and performing in plays
   c responding to performances.

Key Stages 3 and 4

En 1 Speaking and Listening

Knowledge, skills and understanding

Drama

4 To participate in a range of drama activities and to evaluate their own and others' contributions, pupils should be taught to:
   a use a variety of dramatic techniques to explore ideas, issues, texts, meanings
   b use different ways to convey action, character, atmosphere and tension when they are scripting and performing in plays (for example, through dialogue, movement, pace)
   c appreciate how the structure and organisation of scenes and plays contribute to dramatic effect
   d evaluate critically performance of dramas that they have watched or in which they have taken part.

Breadth of study: Drama activities

11 The range should include:
   a improvisation and working in role
   b devising, scripting and performing plays
   c discussing and reviewing their own and others' performances.

Figure 10.4 Drama in the National Curriculum.

appropriate' after the statement 'teachers should teach standard English'. Government documentation now suggests that children should be taught Standard English in all key stages. The higher-level descriptors in En 1 suggest that pupils should be confident users of Standard English.

In challenging classrooms, where some pupils are still learning English and many pupils may lack self-confidence, the teacher must accept, as a starting point, the language that children bring with them to school. Indeed this should be the approach in any classroom. The teacher who listens to and values all their pupils' attempts to communicate will build up relationships in which different forms of talk begin to flourish.

Informal, personal conversations are where we must begin. In these conversations pupils begin to reformulate past experiences, articulate feelings and opinions and can be led from these more affective forms of talk into tasks where they will be required to use more formal language. As this book has argued throughout, this kind of talk plays an important emotional and psychological role in reaffirming identity and increasing pupils' self-esteem. Storytelling allows pupils to use language in a rich variety of ways as it requires different voices and both formal and more informal language.

To move pupils on to the stage where they are able to use language more impersonally – to generalise, persuade, inform and explain – teachers have to create opportunities and contexts where that language needs to be used.

In the trial exercise some students had to be in role as lawyers. In order to prepare this, all the children had to consider the language used in a court and prepare a case collaboratively for the defence or the prosecution. This meant that when the roles of lawyer were chosen many more pupils volunteered than would normally be the case because they felt confident about the type of language they would need to use and the lawyer role made the use of that kind of formal language both necessary and appropriate. The teacher as judge also modelled the language to scaffold the speech of the pupils playing roles in the trial. Witnesses could use colloquial language, as it was appropriate for their roles. Those with the most power in the court used formal language. Those with the least power used colloquial language. This teaches pupils how Standard and non-Standard English works in real-life situations. In this way, the teacher can ensure that all pupils have opportunities to demonstrate their ability to recognise and use Standard English in appropriate situations in order to fulfil the requirements in the level descriptors for En 1.

Using multi-media resources

This takes the assessment of oral work onto another level and helps us to look to the future of English teaching. Many of these devices make talk less transient and therefore make the process of assessing and evaluating oral work easier. The new technologies also allow students to bring a wide range of skills into the classroom that are often under-utilised in English lessons.

- A simple device for assessment is the *tape recorder/dictaphone*. This has been used for evaluating and assessing independent group discussion and group simulations for several decades and it is still an important device which the teacher can use.
- *PowerPoint/interactive whiteboards/video clips* can be used to lend detail and visual/oral stimulus to the spoken word in an individual or group presentation.
- *OHTs* can be used for similar purposes.
- *Video, camcorders and software packages such as moviemaker* can be used to film any oral or drama exercise or to present photo-stories and short films. The teacher or pupils may wish to present these on the CD player or interactive whiteboard.
- *Cameras* can also be used to record, for example, drama exercises such as still image to capture key moments, moods, feelings.
- *Large pieces of paper and coloured pens* are also useful resources to create pictures, posters, diagrams and to annotate work which can be used as evidence of achievement in group work and oral work.

Keeping records

Record keeping in schools is often enormously time consuming and not always purposeful for classroom teachers. Consequently records sometimes remain incomplete or get mislaid. The key skill in record keeping is to think about the purpose of your records and focus only on keeping the marks you really need to use later. Some suggestions might therefore include:

- using the pupils to help you collect evidence of oral work. When you are planning to carry group work on from one lesson to another try to remember to get one pupil to write down the names of the group and place any notes in a folder for the next lesson. In challenging classrooms pupils will not necessarily help you reconstitute the groups and you need your own records to ensure continuity.

- using pupil evaluations, records or logs is a relatively simple, user-friendly method of assessing oral work which can be used for pupils in Key States 2, 3 and 4. Pupil evaluations help with record keeping because they can be used to record the exercise and the role the pupil played. Re-reading them will always remind the teacher of that particular exercise.

- using the completed grids for Key Stages 2, 3 and 4 for your notes on group work or on individual pupils. These grids can also be used at Key Stage 4 by all staff to provide evidence of the three assessments required for the En 1 grade to supplement the GCSE coursework forms. As you use these criteria in the different key stages, you will become more familiar and confident about assessing oral work.

- keeping results of whole class evaluations and your notes in a folder. The adult/pupil observer notes can also be kept in this folder, with dates, as evidence.

- making sure that tapes, videos and photographs are clearly labelled and dated. Ask pupils to print out their PowerPoint for you and keep copies of presentation notes until the end of the year.

- using the register to keep a record of the important assessment moments. The assessment of oral work can easily be included in a hand-written or electronic register. Teachers are often told to record too much and the skill in record keeping is to focus only on recording what you really need to. The teacher can turn the pages of the register or create some extra columns, put a date and a title for the assessment and list the marks or levels in the appropriate column.

Exams at age 16

Twenty per cent of the English Key Stage 4 marks are allocated to speaking and listening and future exams are likely to incorporate such an assessment strand. The mark is no longer awarded separately but it informs the overall grade. The plan of evaluation, record keeping and assessment outlined in these two chapters fits easily with the requirements of the Key Stage 4 syllabus. In Year 11 the teacher simply uses the pupil evaluations and the marks in the register and picks out the assignments that cover the criteria for the exams, which now fall into the three categories of individual presentation, group work or drama. If the teacher has planned for speaking and listening or drama assignments each half-term, they will have plenty of assignments to choose from and will easily cover the type of task and will have matched the skills required.

Oral response to literature

The Assessment and Qualifications Alliance (AQA) GCSE allows pupils to respond orally to one literature assignment as part of their coursework for English literature. This is not just assessment of talk but assessment through talk. In challenging settings, success in this assignment can really motivate students who have difficulty with writing and those who enjoy oral tasks. It is an opportunity for the pupils to talk through an essay with questions and prompts from the teacher. This has the added benefit of teaching the pupils how to write an essay as you prompt their thoughts and references.

In all-boy settings, for example, oral response to literature can be planned as a whole class assignment. Many of the suggestions made earlier in this book could be adapted to cover this component of the literature coursework where pupils have to show understanding (GCSE Grade D) or insight (GCSE Grade C) or analyse and interpret (GCSE Grade A) a literary text. You need to encourage the pupils to discuss, for example, the social and historical context and language of the text and refer directly to the text. You can use the GCSE criteria to plan your questions.

Different formats for eliciting pupil responses could be:

- One-to-one discussion or interview with the teacher
- Small group discussion or interview with the teacher
- Presentation to the class
- Hot-seat as the author/playwright
- Directing the dramatised version of a particular extract.

The English teachers and departments that have built this component into their Key Stage 4 course seem to be very positive about this experience. It is yet another space where the pupils' oral abilities have been given some formal recognition and this does seem to allow for a wider range of pupils to succeed. This assessment experience has an empowering impact on the pupils.

The approach to assessing talk described in this chapter is based on finding out what children can do, what they already know about spoken language and building on and developing their skills. Summative assessments are made only at the end of a series of formative assessments. The pupil is given the chance to succeed by making expectations clear. If teachers were trained and encouraged to use this approach to planning and assessing talk throughout the child's school life the pupils would become very confident listeners and speakers. Adopting even part of this approach to planning for and assessing talk would enrich not only English teaching but also the teaching of many subjects other than English (Coultas, 2006a).

Chapter 11

Training teachers for talk

> England especially has become a testbed for this top-down
> effectiveness-driven version of improvement . . . there is increasing
> pressure towards transmission teaching and replication learning.
>
> Wrigley (2002)

Some of the advice given by supporters of school improvement suggests
that change in schools must come from the top. To a certain extent there
is some validity in this view. The more the whole school, for example,
values speaking and listening and encourages staff to use small group
exploratory talk, the easier it is for the individual teacher to use these
techniques successfully. A policy on speaking and listening and small
group work or a system for auditing the curriculum to assess how
embedded speaking and listening is across all subjects must always be
welcome. If the head teacher is really enthusiastic and knowledgeable
about teaching and learning and how to improve the experience of staff
and students in the classroom, time will be allocated for discussion of
these issues and money and resources will be made available for staff
training.

It is sometimes the case, however, that a more common-sense understanding of the need for good school leaders is transformed into a
tighter, more prescriptive managerial formula. This formula, transferred
from the private sector, suggests that change has to be led from the top
and sold to or imposed on those below through, for example, the school
development plan and performance management targets. In this model,
innovation and creative vision is assumed to come primarily from the
head and the senior team.

This approach obscures an underlying reality of teaching. The classroom is the key entity within the school and it is what happens here, on a

daily basis, that matters most of all. In fact, even above results, it could be suggested that the quality of relationships between the staff and the pupils is the most important indicator of a 'good' school. This is what attracts the best teachers to the profession. This is what parents look for when choosing schools for their children. This is what helps children learn and feel valued.

A much higher proportion of classroom teachers and learning assistants are female. A much higher proportion of higher managers in schools are still male. In much of modern school improvement theory, qualitative factors such as good relationships are downplayed and the male managerial quantitative view predominates. A good school is becoming more and more defined by results not by relationships. Although this top-down model comes from the male-dominated world of business and government departments, it does not mean that all male teachers agree with it while some women in higher managerial posts are, of course, quite willing to subscribe to it.

A quantitative approach, however, implies that rigour lies with numbers – we must set targets, we must monitor schools and teachers to make them more accountable, and we must make teaching more technical, scientific and consistent. We must control the 'delivery' of the curriculum through detailed objectives for every year, every term and every key stage. ICT has been utilised to ensure tighter monitoring from outside schools. Ofsted can now use interactive PANDAS (PANDAS are data used to compare schools in similar situations which can now be accessed through ICT programmes) rather than direct classroom observations, to search out the weak teachers, the weak schools, the weak departments and drive up standards. There is little initiative left to the classroom teacher in this model. Words such as collaboration, sharing, discussion, relationships, evaluation and reflection are not the dominant language of this discourse.

An alternative approach to how change takes place in schools is based on the view that change does not always come from the top; that the classroom teacher, who has a degree, and a post-graduate qualification in many instances, can be creative, innovative, that *she* can and often does develop pedagogies to engage the pupils she teaches. Teachers also refine, develop and transform advice from above to ensure that their pupils' needs are met and that the motivation to learn is kept intact. Many teachers also believe that local communities, parents and pupils can and should influence the curriculum. Many believe that this is the most important way a school should be accountable, by listening to the needs and concerns of the pupils, the staff and the local community.

The teachers who are sensitive to the cultural, religious and linguistic traditions of those they teach have often been at the forefront of change and innovation, long before those at the top realised that curriculum change was needed. The process that informs this form of change is not the drive to raise standards, although this may be an indirect effect, but the process of building good relationships, sharing good practice and establishing collaboration between different teams and groups from within the school community to improve life in schools. It recognises that most teachers want to teach well, that all teachers are managers of complex organisations, the classroom, and that the best teaching teams work on an equal rather than a hierarchical basis.

This view of teachers working together to empower each other is a different approach to the more managerial stance outlined above. Teachers sharing ideas with one another, as reflective practitioners, also encourages them to approach classroom teaching in a more democratic spirit and helps them to recognise the role of the pupils in evaluating teaching approaches.

In fact, change that comes from below often has a more lasting impact. Practices that staff discover and disseminate among themselves have been tried out in real contexts and often help the teacher to do their job more effectively. Change that is imposed from above can often have the opposite effect, wasting huge amounts of money and making the classroom teacher's job more difficult by imposing unnecessary paperwork. For example, overelaborate ICT systems of assessment can become far too complex for any teacher to really use or any parent to understand. The role of LEA advisory teachers, prior to the rise of the 'consultants', was often to create opportunities for schools to share good practice.

The best head teachers, however, those who still see themselves as educationalists, and staff trainers, still seek out what is good in a school, celebrate it and share it with others. They view change from above critically and select the advice that is useful to their particular context.

A more sensitive approach to staff development can have a very positive impact on staff morale and help to create a mutually supportive team in any school. Schools that are facing 'challenging circumstances', where social disadvantage is commonplace, need this team-based approach more than any other school. To deal with the daily challenges such a school brings, you need all the staff to work together to stop the fights quickly, to be willing to be on rotas at break, lunch and after school, to be ready to meet and greet the pupils, to be available for one-to-one discussions with pupils. But also you need a team approach to successfully adapt the curriculum so that it meets the needs and engages the intellects of the pupils who attend that school. Through collaboration and debate about teaching and learning, teachers in schools such as these have to be given the opportunities, the time and the support to be creative.

Heads do not have to follow a narrowly managerial agenda. They can refuse to use performance management to promote new hierarchies that undermine staff teams and choose instead to focus on the training aspects of yearly reviews for individuals and keep pay in the school as egalitarian as possible. They can encourage teams to audit their teaching plans and schemes to focus on, for example, speaking and listening, literacy, special needs or higher-order skills, and allocate INSET days to these tasks, to encourage teams to evaluate and review their teaching and share good practice. Peer reviews, where staff nominate a colleague to watch them teach, can take place in informal circumstances where the emphasis is placed on sharing skills and less on making final judgements. When staff are being encouraged to plan for small group learning it is particularly obvious that a top down training model is inappropriate.

This chapter will focus on staff training where a non-hierarchical approach is taken and where the aim is to share good practice, confront real problems, increase teaching repertoires and boost staff morale. This approach has been used very successfully in schools in challenging circumstances where staff retention and recruitment is often a key problem and good training on the job is essential.

Two examples of INSET sessions around speaking and listening have been chosen, from the experience of working in one such school, where staff were closely involved in planning, delivering and evaluating the training. For example, in the planning stage, staff were involved in trying out some new approaches with the support of the teacher in charge of Continuing Professional Development (CPD). On the day, these staff would describe and evaluate the new approaches. Where the behaviour of the pupils is particularly challenging, the authenticity of the trainers is often an issue. Staff need to be convinced that these new ideas work in a particular context or they will be sceptical of the advice given. Home-grown expertise can be very valuable in these settings. If outside expertise is used it is often useful if the trainers come in to the school and work with staff and pupils before the training day to gain more understanding of the context. All these sessions use the idea of a training loop where all or key parts of the session are modelling the kind of practice that could be used in the classroom.

Workshop for training a team: planning for small group learning in the classroom

This approach could be used with a department or small group of teachers, e.g. newly qualified teachers or staff involved in teaching a particular subject. The workshop was based on the theories of small group learning promoted by the National Oracy Project which have informed the overall approach of this book. The training loop was made explicit at the end of the session.

Engagement: stage 1

The session began by asking the staff to consider a lesson or series of lessons where they had encouraged the pupils to work collaboratively, in pairs or groups. It was then suggested that they try to break up the process of teaching into particular stages. How would they describe them?

Exploration: stage 2

The trainer then modelled an example of small group work using the example of freeze-frame and interior monologue in a scene from *A View from the Bridge*, outlined in Chapter 6. One group was invited to perform the play and the whole group evaluated the activity and discussed the use of such an exercise in the classroom.

The group were then introduced to the National Oracy Project model of learning in small groups through a diagram and a description of each stage (see p. 5). A chart (see Figure 11.1) was handed to them in pairs and they considered whether this example would fit into the stages listed.

- Was it necessary to use all these stages in planning for small group work?
- Were the stages useful?
- Why?
- Had they found anything else useful in planning for small group work?

The trainer then handed out a few difficult scenarios for discussion in groups (see Figure 11.2). The staff had to decide what to do in each situation and then a list was compiled of problems that might be confronted when attempting small group work.

Engagement This is when students encounter new information or material	
Exploration This is when students explore that new information	
Transformation Students are required to use their understanding to work with the information to make decisions	
Presentation The students present their findings to an interested audience	
Reflection Students look at what they have learned and the process they have gone through	
Notes/Comments	

Figure 11.1 A model for small group learning – grid for staff training.

Source: This table is derived from information found in Cook, J, Forrestral, P, Reid, J (1989) *Small Group Learning in the Classroom* Chalkface Press.

Transformation: stage 3

The trainer discussed some of the key issues involved in establishing successful group work, e.g. classroom ethos, the need for careful planning and ground rules for talk to ensure that the groups worked well. The group was then divided into two smaller groups. Group A was asked to produce on a large sheet some ground rules for talk in challenging classrooms (see Figure 11.3). Group B was asked to produce an *aide-mémoire* for teachers when planning for talk, again on a large sheet (see Figure 11.4).

Scenario 1: Late from PE
The class arrives late from PE. It's hot. Three or four pupils have been winding each other up en route to your lesson. The lesson begins reasonably well. The pupils move into groups. The 'challenging group' are not listening and do not move. The rest of the class is busy getting on with the task. What do you do?

Scenario 2: Off-task talk
You have not been teaching the class all year. You have had them for one term. The class loved their previous teacher. The pupils are working well in pairs and you now ask the twos to become fours. Some pairs are reluctant to join the group and are very slow to move. When they are eventually persuaded to move they keep talking off task. What do you do?

Scenario 3: Getting them into groups
You have established a procedure for organising group discussion in a Jigsaw. You give pupils a number from 1 to 5 and ask them to write it down in their books and to get ready to move into specialist groups. You then go through the group numbers 1 to 5 and ask all the pupils to raise their hands if they have been assigned to that group. You intend to appoint a named person as a group leader for each group.
    You start with group 1 and a smaller number than expected raise their hands. You know some pupils are trying to undermine the groupings. What do you do?

Scenario 4: Who belongs where?
You set up an oral activity and you expect it to be completed in one lesson but the pupils want to carry on with the task. You have failed to keep a record of which pupils are in each group and when the next lesson begins the pupils start arguing about who goes where. They realise you are confused and begin to enjoy adding to your confusion. What do you do?

Figure 11.2 Scenarios.

Presentation/report back: stage 4

The group was asked to sit in a circle next to someone in a different group to them. The teachers were then asked to explain to each other what they had done.

Reflection: stage 5

The trainer highlighted the fact that the workshop had itself followed the National Oracy Project model of learning in small groups. The participants then answered the following questions, on their own at first and then as part of a whole group discussion.

Rationale:

Some suggestions for ground rules:

-
-
-
-
-
-

Figure 11.3 Ground rules for talk – *aide-mémoire*.

Rationale:

Points to consider:

-
-
-
-
-
-

Figure 11.4 Planning for talk in small groups – *aide-mémoire*.

1   What have I learnt?
2   How do I feel about being trained like this?
3   How does this connect with my existing practice in the classroom?
4   In what ways will this session influence my teaching in the future?

Twilight session for whole staff training: oracy across the curriculum

This session took place as the first on Cross-curricular Literacy when the NLS framework was introduced at Key Stage 3. The emphasis here was to give staff a background knowledge of some past debates on speaking and listening in order for them to understand why this was such an important aspect of literacy and a child's language development. The emphasis was on how small group collaborative learning could support EAL pupils and pupils with special needs. The session also aimed to explain the relevance of speaking and listening to all subjects and to demonstrate some practical examples of how it could be used in different lessons as an introduction to the cross-curricular themes in the Key Stage 3 documentation.

Stage 1

A speaker, from within the school, gave a talk on oracy and the social nature of language, how it played such an important part in children's learning, literacy and language development and why small group collaborative talk was particularly important for pupils with EAL and special needs.

Stage 2

A short summary of the story of *Macbeth* was handed to the staff. They had to carry out the one-minute storytelling exercise described in Chapter 5. This involved reading the summary and then telling the story to a colleague in five minutes. The storyteller then had to change and tell the story in three minutes. Finally, one partner was asked to tell the story in one minute. The staff were then asked what they enjoyed about this activity, what pupils might enjoy and what they would be learning. How would such an activity prepare EAL and SEN pupils for reading the play?

Stage 3: workshops

Three workshops took place on the following three aspects of planning for talk:

1   Planning for small group collaborative learning (the workshop was led by an RE and English teacher)
    The teachers explained how they had planned an RE lesson on abortion where each group had to put the moral case for or against abortion. The notes that supported each group in preparing the discussion were shown and the RE teacher explained that he was impressed by the way in which a class with many EAL pupils had

managed to make their case quite clearly as a result of the small group preparation.

2   Planning for a Jigsaw activity (the workshop was led by a history teacher)

The teacher explained how he had planned a Jigsaw activity for groups to adopt the roles of the different participants in the Peasant's Revolt, e.g. peasants, landlords, the Church and the king, and then join together as a panel to put their different views at the end.

3   Planning for role play (the workshop was led by an MFL teacher)

The teacher discussed how he planned for role play in French conversation in simple situations such as buying a ticket, ordering a meal or introducing yourself to a new friend.

Stage 3 evaluation

The staff were asked to fill in their normal evaluation sheet (see Figure 11.5). This sheet was very quick and easy to complete and the response was very positive. This was one of the most popular training sessions over a two-year period. The staff really felt that they had learnt something that was new and of practical use in the classroom.

Course Title: ....

Date: ....

Which aspects of the course were most useful?

Which aspects of the course were least useful?

Which term sums up your feelings about the event?
(Please tick)

Very worthwhile	Worthwhile	Neutral	Not very worthwhile	Not at all worthwhile

Please use this space for comments including further suggestions for INSET.

Figure 11.5 Staff INSET evaluation form.

A follow up

There was a follow up to this session. First, the teacher in charge of staff development volunteered to visit classrooms to plan, team-teach or observe staff implementing some of these ideas. Second, a further session looked at using video to record and evaluate pupil presentations. This was very successful, as a recording from a French lesson demonstrated how confident some African pupils were at speaking French, their mother tongue, and how this model had inspired monolingual pupils to become more confident about attempting to speak French.

These two examples demonstrate that using the staff in the school to train and share good practice is an effective approach to training. There were none of the usual cynical remarks in these sessions. Staff did not question the relevance of the techniques and were interested in how to apply the strategies in their subject. In the former session, the experience of the staff was used at the very beginning of the session. In the latter session, the experience of the staff was used in evaluating the storytelling exercise and through being allowed to interrogate the planned activities in the workshop.

Very importantly, however, staff involvement before the oracy session meant that the ideas had already been piloted and teachers were able to see how successful these teaching techniques could be in their own classrooms. The storytelling and drama activities were greatly enjoyed and carefully evaluated. Once you as a teacher understand that language is, as the social constructivists argue, 'a tool for thought' and you know how small group collaboration inspires pupils, you can see how collaboration can and should empower teachers.

Poetry and literature cited in the text

Agard, J (1998) Half-Caste in *NEAB Anthology English and English Literature* Heinemann

Amery, H (1999) *Greek Myths for Young Children* Usborne

Armitage, H (1998) Untitled Poem in *NEAB Anthology English and English Literature* Heinemann

Bloom, V (1996) Wha Fe Call I in *NEAB Anthology English and English Literature* Heinemann

Brock, J (1991) *Charles Dickens' Oliver Twist* Samuel French Ltd

Burningham, H (2002) *The Graphic Shakespeare Series, Macbeth* Evans Brothers Ltd

Dahl, R (2000) Lamb to the Slaughter in *Skin and Other Stories* Penguin

Dickens, C (1996) *Great Expectations* Penguin

Forsyth, B (2001) *Gregory's Girl* London: Cinema Club. Original film release 1981

Garfield, L (1992) *Shakespeare, The Animated Tales* Heinemann Young Books

Gibson, R (1993) *Cambridge School Shakespeare, Macbeth* Cambridge University Press

Golding, W (2005) *Lord of the Flies* Faber and Faber

Lamb, C and Lamb, M (1996) *Tales from Shakespeare* Dent

McGough, R (1976) *The Lesson in the Glass Room* Cape

Magorian, M (1981) *Goodnight Mr Tom* Penguin

Miller, A (1977) *A View from the Bridge* Penguin

Morpurgo, M (1999) *Kensuke's Kingdom* Egmont

Shakespeare, W (1968) *The Tempest* Penguin Books

Smucker, B (1986) *Underground to Canada* Puffin Books

Voznesensky, A (1985) First Ice in *New Russian Poets* Marion Boyars

Bibliography

Alexander, R (2000) *Culture and Pedagogy* Blackwell
—— (2004) Talking to Learn *TES* 30 January
Allen, N (2002) Too Much, Too Young? An Analysis of the Key Stage 3 Literacy Strategy in Practice *English in Education* Vol. 36 No. 1 Spring
Barnes, D, Britton, J and Rosen, H (1969) *Language, the Learner and the School* Penguin
Barrs, M and Cork, V (2001) *The Reader in the Writer, Case Studies in Children's Writing* CLPE
Benn, C (2001) A Credible Alternative: Some Tasks for the Future, *Education and Social Justice* Vol. 3 No. 2 Spring
Bennet, R (2004) *Using ICT in Primary English Teaching* Learning Matters
Bloom, B (1990) Bloom's Taxonomy, cited by Robeck, M and Wallace, R, 2nd revised edition, in *The Psychology of Reading* Laurence Erlbaum
Bowell, P and Heap, S (2001) *Planning Process Drama* David Fulton
British Film Institute (2001) *Starting Stories* BFI Education
—— (2003) *Look Again. A Teaching Guide to Using Film and Television with 3–11 Year Olds* BFI Education
Britton, J (1972) *Language and Learning* Penguin
Bruner, J (1986) *Actual Minds, Possible Worlds* Harvard University Press
—— (1996) *The Culture of Education* Harvard University Press
Bunting, R (2000) *Teaching about Language in the Primary Years* David Fulton
Carter, R and McCarthy, M (1997) *Exploring Spoken English* Cambridge University Press
Chang, G and Wells, G (1988) The Literate Potential of Collaborative Talk in Maclure, M, Phillips T and Wilkinson, A (eds) *Oracy Matters* Open University Press
Cook, J, Forrestral, P and Reid, J (1989) *Small Group Learning in the Classroom* Chalkface Press
Corden, R (1988) *Talk about Oral Skills in Context* Stanley Thornes

—— (2000) *Literacy and Learning through Talk: Strategies for the Primary Classroom* Open University Press

Coultas, V (2003) Becoming a Creative Teacher in Cole, M (ed) 2nd edn *Professional Values and Practice* David Fulton

—— (2006a) Thinking Out of the SATS box – Assessment through Talk *Drama and English Magazine* NATE

—— (2006b) Investigating Talk in Challenging Classrooms – Boys Enjoy the Power of Talk *English in Education* Summer

Cowley, S (2004) *Getting the Buggers to Think* Continuum

Cox, B (1991) *Cox on Cox: An English Curriculum for the 1990s* Hodder and Stoughton

—— (1996) *Cox on the Battle for the English Curriculum* Hodder and Stoughton

Crawford, M (1995) *Talking Difference: On Gender and Language* Sage Publications

Davidson, J (2004) cited by A Shepherd in ILEA planted a passion in me *TES* 7 May

DES (1967) *Children and their Primary Schools (Plowden Report)* HMSO

—— (1975) *A Language for Life. Report of the Committee of Enquiry chaired by Sir Allan Bullock* HMSO

—— (1988) *Report of the Committee of Inquiry into the Teaching of the English Language (Kingman Report)* HMSO

—— (1990) *English in the National Curriculum* HMSO

—— (1995) *English in the National Curriculum* HMSO

DFES (1998) *The National Literacy Strategy. Framework for Teaching* Cambridge University Press

—— (2003a) *Drama in the Key Stage 3 English Framework* DFES Publications

—— (2003b) *Excellence and Enjoyment. A Strategy for Primary Schools* DFES Publications

—— (2003c) *Key Stage 3 National Strategy: Key Messages: Pedagogy and Practice* DFES Publications

—— (2003d) *The Key Stage 3 Strategy, Teaching and Learning in Secondary Schools: Pilot* Cambridge University Press

Unit 4: Questioning
Unit 5: Active Engagement Strategies
Unit 6: Starters and Plenaries
Unit 7: Group Work
Unit 9: Improving the Climate for Learning

—— (2003e) *The Primary National Strategy. Speaking and Listening at Key Stages 1 and 2* DFES Publications

Dixon, N, Davies, A and Politano, C (1996) *Learning with Reader's Theatre* Peguis Publishers

English Speaking Union (2003a) *Get debating!* ESU

—— (2003b) *Debate in the Curriculum Teaching Resource* ESU

Firth, G (1987) 'The time of your life': the Meaning of the School Story in Arnot, M and Weiner, G (eds) *Gender Under Scrutiny. New Enquiries in Education* Open University Press

Frater, G (1988) Oracy in England – A New Tide: An HMI Overview in Phillips, T, Maclure, M and Wilkinson, A (eds) *Oracy Matters* Open University Press

Gilbert, F (2004) *I'm a Teacher, Get Me Out of Here* Short Books

Grahame, J (1991) *The English Curriculum: Media 1 7–9* English and Media Centre

Grainger, T (2003) Crick, Crack Chin my Story's in in Goodwin, P (ed) *The Articulate Classroom* David Fulton

HMI (2005) English 2000–5, *A Review of the Inspection Evidence* [Crown copyright] OFSTED

Hunt, G (2001) Talking about Reading in Goodwin, P (ed) *The Articulate Classroom* David Fulton

Jones, P (1988) *Lipservice: The Story of Talk in Schools* Open University Press

Jones, K (1989) *Right Turn. The Conservative Revolution in Education* Hutchinson Radius

Marland, M (1991) *The Craft of the Classroom – A Survival Guide* Heinemann

Mercer, N (2000) *Words and Minds* Routledge

Moore, R and Bunyan, P (2005) *NATE Drama Pack, Drama within English at KS 3 and 4* Q3 Digital/Litho

Moss, G (2004) Changing Practice: The National Literacy Strategy and the Politics of Literacy Policy *UKLA 2004* Blackwell Publishing

NATE (2005) *Submission to English 21*

Norman, K (ed) (2002) *Thinking Voices – The Work of the National Oracy Project* Hodder and Stoughton

QCA (2003) *New Perspectives on Spoken English*, QCA

Reynolds, P (1991) *Practical Approaches to Shakespeare* Oxford University Press

Riley, J and Elmer, C (2001) Survey of the Literacy Hour *Primary English Magazine* Vol. 7, No. 1

Russell, W (1991) in Hughes, V *Literature Belongs to Everyone* London: Arts Council

Simms, L (1982) *Storytelling, Children and Imagination* The Yarnspinner Series 6(2) Heinemann

Smith, F and Hardman, F (2000) Evaluating the Effectiveness of the National Literacy Strategy *Educational Studies* Vol. 26, No. 3

Stanworth, M (1987) Girls on the Margins: a Study of Gender Divisions in the Classroom in Weiner, G and Arnot, M (eds) *Gender Under Scrutiny. New Enquiries in Education* Hutchinson

Stephens, J and Simmons, M (1990) *School* English and Media Centre

Tough, J (1973) *Focus on Meaning* Unwin Education

Thomas, P (2001) The Pleasure and Power of the Paragraph *Secondary English Magazine* January

Vygotsky, L (1986) *Thought and Language* MIT Press

Webster, L (2004) *Studying Great Expectations, EMC Study Guide* English and Media Centre

Wilkinson, A (1965) *Spoken English* University of Birmingham

Wilson, A (2001) *Language Knowledge for Primary Teachers* David Fulton

Wrigley, T (2002) Class, Culture and Curriculum: Critical Issues for School Improvement *Education and Social Justice* Vol. 4 No. 3 Trentham Books

Wyse, D and Jones, R (2001) *Teaching English, Language and Literacy in the Primary School* RoutledgeFalmer

Audiovisual

Stanislov, S (1999) *Shakespeare, The Animated Tales (The Tempest)* Shakespeare Animated Films Ltd & Soyuzmult Film

Websites

www.aqua.org.uk

www.collaborativelearning.com

www.nate.org.uk

Index